SUNDAY
in the
PARK
with
GEORGE

SUNDAY in the PARK with GEORGE

A Musical

Music and Lyrics by
STEPHEN SONDHEIM

Book by
JAMES LAPINE

ILLUSTRATED WITH PHOTOGRAPHS

DODD, MEAD & COMPANY, *New York*

Book copyright © 1986 by James Lapine
Lyrics copyright © 1984 by Revelation Music Publishing Corp.
and Rilting Music, Inc. Used by special permission.

Published by Dodd, Mead & Company, Inc.
79 Madison Avenue, New York, N.Y. 10016
Distributed in Canada by
McClelland and Stewart Limited, Toronto
Manufactured in the United States of America
Designed by Helen Winfield
FIRST EDITION

CAUTION: Professionals and amateurs are hereby warned that *Sunday in the Park with George*, being fully protected under the Copyright Laws of the United States of America and all other countries of the Berne and Universal Copyright Conventions, is subject to royalty. All rights, including but not limited to, professional, amateur, recording, motion picture, recitation, lecturing, public reading, radio and television broadcasting, and the rights of translation into foreign languages are strictly reserved, permission for which must be secured in writing from the Authors' agents, Flora Roberts, Inc. (for Stephen Sondheim), 157 West 57th Street, New York, New York 10019, and William Morris Agency, Inc. (for James Lapine), 1350 Avenue of the Americas, New York, New York 10019, Attn: George Lane.

All photographs, unless otherwise credited, courtesy of and copyright 1985 by Martha Swope

Library of Congress Cataloging-in-Publication Data

Sondheim, Stephen.
[Sunday in the park with George. Libretto]
Sunday in the park with George.

Libretto.
1. Musical reviews, comedies, etc.—Librettos.
2. Seurat, Georges, 1859–1891—Drama.   I. Lapine, James.
II. Title.
ML50.S705S8 1986   782.81'2   85-27473
Trade Edition: ISBN 0-396-08600-4
Limited Edition: ISBN 0-396-08897-X

For Sarah Kernochan

Sunday in the Park with George was first presented by The Shubert Organization and Emanuel Azenberg, by arrangement with Playwrights Horizons, at the Booth Theatre on May 2, 1984, with the following cast (in order of appearance):

ACT I

GEORGE, *an artist* .... Mandy Patinkin
DOT, *his mistress*..................... Bernadette Peters
AN OLD LADY........................... Barbara Bryne
HER NURSE............................. Judith Moore
FRANZ, *a servant* .... Brent Spiner
A BOY *bathing in the river* .... Danielle Ferland
A YOUNG MAN *sitting on the bank*............. Nancy Opel
A MAN *lying on the bank* .... Cris Groenendaal
JULES, *another artist* .... Charles Kimbrough
YVONNE, *his wife* .... Dana Ivey
A BOATMAN .... William Parry
CELESTE #1......................... Melanie Vaughan
CELESTE #2............................ Mary D'Arcy
LOUISE, *the daughter of Jules and Yvonne*...Danielle Ferland
FRIEDA, *a cook*........................... Nancy Opel
LOUIS, *a baker* .... Cris Groenendaal
A SOLDIER .... Robert Westenberg
A MAN *with bicycle* .... John Jellison
A LITTLE GIRL......................... Michele Rigan
A WOMAN *with baby carriage* .... Sue Anne Gershenson
MR. .... Kurt Knudson
MRS. .... Judith Moore

ACT II

GEORGE, *an artist* .... Mandy Patinkin
MARIE, *his grandmother* .... Bernadette Peters
DENNIS, *a technician*..................... Brent Spiner
BOB GREENBERG, *the museum director* .. Charles Kimbrough
NAOMI EISEN, *a composer* .... Dana Ivey
HARRIET PAWLING, *a patron of the arts*...... Judith Moore
BILLY WEBSTER, *her friend* .... Cris Groenendaal
A PHOTOGRAPHER .... Sue Anne Gershenson
A MUSEUM ASSISTANT.................... John Jellison
CHARLES REDMOND, *a visiting curator*....... William Parry
ALEX, *an artist*...................... Robert Westenberg
BETTY, *an artist*...........................Nancy Opel
LEE RANDOLPH, *the museum's publicist* ...... Kurt Knudson
BLAIR DANIELS, *an art critic* .... Barbara Bryne
A WAITRESS ....Melanie Vaughan
ELAINE ....Mary D'Arcy

Directed by James Lapine
Scenery by Tony Straiges
Costumes by Patricia Zipprodt and Ann Hould-Ward
Lighting by Richard Nelson
Special Effects by Bran Ferren
Movement by Randolyn Zinn
Sound by Tom Morse
Orchestrations by Michael Starobin
Musical Direction by Paul Gemignani
Production Stage Manager: Charles Blackwell
Stage Manager: Fredric H. Orner
Assistant Stage Manager: Loretta Robertson

MUSICAL NUMBERS

ACT I

"Sunday in the Park with George" . . . . DOT
"No Life" . . . . JULES, YVONNE
"Color and Light" . . . . DOT, GEORGE
"Gossip" . . . . CELESTE #1, CELESTE #2,
BOATMAN, NURSE, OLD
LADY, JULES, YVONNE
"The Day Off" . . . . GEORGE, NURSE, FRANZ,
FRIEDA, BOATMAN,
SOLDIER, CELESTE #1,
CELESTE #2, YVONNE,
LOUISE, JULES, LOUIS
"Everybody Loves Louis" . . . . DOT
"Finishing the Hat" . . . . GEORGE
"We Do Not Belong Together" . . . . DOT, GEORGE
"Beautiful" . . . . OLD LADY, GEORGE
"Sunday" . . . . COMPANY

ACT II

"It's Hot Up Here" . . . . COMPANY
"Chromolume #7" . . . . GEORGE, MARIE
"Putting It Together" . . . . GEORGE, COMPANY

9

The first act of *Sunday in the Park with George* was presented by Playwrights Horizons (Andre Bishop, Artistic Director, Paul Daniels, Managing Director, Ira Weitzman, Musical Theatre Program Director) in association with the Herrick Theatre Foundation, in a workshop production at Playwrights Horizons on July 9, 1983, with the following cast:

GEORGE, *an artist*	Mandy Patinkin
DOT, *his mistress*	Bernadette Peters
OLD LADY	Carmen Mathews
NURSE	Judith Moore
FRANZ, *a coachman*	Brent Spiner
BOY *in the water*	Bradley Kane
YOUNG MAN *on the bank*	Kelsey Grammer
PERVERT	William Parry
LOUISE, *a little girl*	Danielle Ferland
JULES, *another artist*	Ralph Byers
CLARISSE, *his wife*	Christine Baranski
BOATMAN	William Parry
LOUIS, *a baker*	Kevin Marcum
CELESTE 1, *a shopgirl*	Melanie Vaughan
CELESTE 2, *another shopgirl*	Mary Elizabeth Mastrantonio
BETTE, *a cook*	Nancy Opel
SOLDIER	Kelsey Grammer
MR.	Kurt Knudson
MRS.	Judith Moore

Directed by James Lapine
Set design by Tony Straiges

11

Costume design by Patricia Zipprodt and Ann Hould-Ward
Lighting design by Richard Nelson
Sound design by Scott Lehrer
Musical direction by Paul Gemignani

MUSICAL NUMBERS

"*Sunday in the Park with George*" . . . . DOT
"*Yoo-Hoo!*" . . . . BOY, YOUNG MAN, PERVERT
"*No Life*" . . . . JULES, CLARISSE
"*Color and Light*" . . . . DOT, GEORGE
"*Gossip*" . . . . CELESTE 1, CELESTE 2,
BOATMAN, NURSE, OLD
LADY, JULES, CLARISSE
"*The Day Off*" . . . . GEORGE, SPOT, FIFI, NURSE,
FRANZ, BETTE, BOATMAN,
SOLDIER, CLARISSE, LOUISE,
CELESTE 1, CELESTE 2
"*Everybody Loves Louis*" . . . . DOT
"*Soldiers and Girls*" . . . . SOLDIER, CELESTE 1,
CELESTE 2
"*Finishing the Hat*" . . . . GEORGE
"*Beautiful*" . . . . OLD LADY, GEORGE
"*Sunday*" . . . . COMPANY

13

Georges Seurat (1859–1891)

The painter Georges Seurat was born in 1859 in Paris and died there in 1891. "Dimanche, Après-Midi à l'Ile de la Grande Jatte" ("A Sunday Afternoon on the Island of La Grande Jatte") was his second major work; it was begun in May 1884 and completed two years later.

The painting measures 81″ × 120″ and was created with thousands of dotlike brushstrokes. It was first shown at the Eighth, and last, Impressionist Exhibition in 1886, and currently hangs at The Art Institute of Chicago.

At the time Seurat painted it, the island of La Grande Jatte was a meeting place frequented primarily by the working class, although fashionable society apparently liked to pay it occasional covert visits.

Sunday in the Park with George is a work of fiction inspired by the art of Seurat and what little is known of his life.

Act I takes place on a series of Sundays from 1884 to 1886 and alternates between a park on an island in the Seine just outside of Paris and George's studio.

Act II takes place in 1984 at an American art museum and on the island.

ACT I

A white stage. White floor, slightly raked and ex-tended in perspective. Four white portals define the space. The proscenium arch continues across the bottom as well, creating a complete frame around the stage.

GEORGE *enters downstage.* HE *is an artist. Tall, dark beard, wearing a soft felt hat with a very narrow brim crushed down at the neck, and a short jacket.* HE *looks rather intense.* HE *sits downstage on the apron at an easel with a large drawing pad and a box of chalk.* HE *stares momentarily at the pad before turning to the audience.*

GEORGE

White. A blank page or canvas. The challenge: bring order to the whole.
    (*Arpeggiated chord. A tree flies in stage right*)
Through design.
    (*Four arpeggiated chords. The white portals fly out and the white ground cloth comes off, revealing a grassy-green expanse and portals depicting the park scene*)
Composition.

(Two arpeggiated chords. A tree tracks on from stage left)

Balance.

      (Two arpeggiated chords. Two trees descend)

Light.

(Arpeggiated chord. The lighting bumps, giving the impression of an early morning sunrise on the island of La Grande Jatte — harsh shadows and streaming golden light through the trees)

And harmony.

(The music coalesces into a theme: "Sunday," as a cut-out of a couple rises at the back of the stage. GEORGE begins to draw, then stops suddenly and goes to the wings and brings on a young woman, DOT. SHE wears a traditional 19th-century outfit: full-length dress with bustle, etc. When HE gets her downstage right, HE turns her profile, then returns downstage to his easel. HE begins to draw. SHE turns to him. Music continues under. Annoyed)

No. Now I want you to look out at the water.

DOT

I feel foolish.

GEORGE

Why?

DOT
(Indicating bustle)

I hate this thing.

GEORGE

Then why wear it?

22

DOT

Why wear it? Everyone is wearing them!

GEORGE
(*Begins sketching*)

Everyone . . .

DOT

You know they are.
(SHE *begins to move*)

GEORGE

Stand still, please.
(*Music stops*)

DOT
(*Sighs*)

I read they're even wearing them in America.

GEORGE

They are fighting Indians in America — and you cannot read.

DOT
(*Defensive*)

I can read . . . a little.
(*Pause*)

Why did we have to get up so early?

GEORGE

The light.

DOT

Oh.

(GEORGE *lets out a moan*)

What's the matter?

GEORGE
(*Erasing feverishly*)

I hate this tree.
(*Arpeggio. A tree rises back into the fly space*)

DOT
(*Hurt*)

I thought you were drawing me.

GEORGE
(*Muttering*)

I am. I am. Just stand still.
(DOT *is oblivious to the moved tree. Through the course
of the scene the landscape can continue to change. At
this point a sailboat begins to slide into view*)

DOT

I wish we could go sailing. I wouldn't go this early in the day,
though.

GEORGE

Could you drop your head a little, please.
(SHE *drops her head completely*)

Dot!
(*She looks up, giggling*)

If you wish to be a good model you must learn to concentrate.
Hold the pose. Look out at the water.
(SHE *obliges*)

Thank you.

(OLD LADY *enters*)

OLD LADY

Where is that tree?

(*Pause*)

NURSE! NURSE!

DOT

(*Startled*)

My God!

(*Sees* OLD LADY)

She is everywhere.

(NURSE *enters.* SHE *wears an enormous headdress*)

OLD LADY

NURSE!

NURSE

What is it, Madame?

OLD LADY

The tree. The tree. Where is our tree?

NURSE

What tree?

OLD LADY

The tree we always sit near. Someone has moved it.

NURSE

No one has moved it, Madame. It is right over there. Now come along —

(NURSE *attempts to help the* OLD LADY *along*)

OLD LADY

Do not push me!

NURSE

I am not pushing. I am helping.

OLD LADY

You are pushing and I do not need any help.

NURSE
(THEY *cross the stage*)

Yes, Madame.

OLD LADY

And this is not our tree!
(SHE *continues her shuffle*)

NURSE

Yes, Madame.
(SHE *helps* OLD LADY *sit in front of tree*)

DOT

I do not envy the nurse.

GEORGE
(*Under his breath*)

She can read . . .

DOT
(*Retaliating*)

They were talking about you at La Coupole.

GEORGE

Oh.

DOT

Saying strange things . . .

26

GEORGE

They have so little to speak of, they must speak of me?

DOT

Were you at the zoo, George?
                    (*No response*)
Drawing the monkey cage?

GEORGE

Not the monkey cage.

DOT

They said they saw you.

GEORGE

The monkeys, Dot. Not the cage.

DOT
                    (*Giggling*)
It is true? Why draw monkeys?

OLD LADY

Nurse, what is that?

NURSE

What, Madame?

OLD LADY
                    (*Points out front*)
That! Off in the distance.

NURSE

They are making way for the exposition.

OLD LADY

What exposition?

NURSE

The International Exposition. They are going to build a tower.

OLD LADY

Another exposition . . .

NURSE

They say it is going to be the tallest structure in the world.

OLD LADY

More foreigners. I am sick of foreigners.

GEORGE

More boats.
          (*An arpeggiated chord. A tugboat appears*)
More trees.
               (*Two chords. More trees track on*)

DOT

George.
               (*Chord*)
Why is it you always get to sit in the shade while I have to stand
in the sun?
               (*Chord. No response*)
George?
               (*Still no response*)
Hello, George?
               (*Chord*)
There is someone in this dress!
               (*Twitches slightly, sings to herself*)

A trickle of sweat.
                    (*Twitch*)
The back of the —
                    (*Twitch*)
—head.
He always does this.
                    (*Hiss*)
Now the foot is dead.
Sunday in the park with George.
One more Su —
                    (*Twitch*)
The collar is damp,
Beginning to pinch.
The bustle's slipping —
                    (*Hiss and twitch*)
I won't budge one inch.

Who was at the zoo, George?
Who was at the zoo?
The monkeys and who, George?
The monkeys and who?

GEORGE

Don't move!

DOT
(*Still*)
Artists are bizarre. Fixed. Cold.
That's you, George, you're bizarre. Fixed. Cold.
I like that in a man. Fixed. Cold.
God, it's hot out here.

Well, there are worse things
Than staring at the water on a Sunday.

There are worse things
Than staring at the water
As you're posing for a picture
Being painted by your lover
In the middle of the summer
On an island in the river on a Sunday.
>   (GEORGE *races over to* DOT *and rearranges her a bit,*
>   *as if* SHE *were an object, then returns to his easel and*
>   *resumes sketching.* DOT *hisses, twitching again*)

The petticoat's wet,
Which adds to the weight.
The sun is blinding.
>   (*Closing her eyes*)

All right, concentrate . . .

GEORGE

Eyes open, please.

DOT

Sunday in the park with George . . .

GEORGE

Look out at the water. Not at me.

DOT

Sunday in the park with George . . .
Concentrate . . . concentrate . . .
>   (*The dress opens and* DOT *walks out of it. The dress*
>   *closes;* GEORGE *continues sketching it as if* SHE *were*
>   *still inside. During the following,* DOT *moves around*
>   *the stage taking representative poses as punctuation to*
>   *the music, which is heavily rhythmic*)

Well, if you want bread

30

And respect
And attention,
Not to say connection,
Modelling's no profession.
(Does mock poses)
If you want instead,
When you're dead,
Some more public
And more permanent
Expression
(Poses)
Of affection,
(Poses)
You want a painter,
(Brief, sharp poses throughout the following)
Poet,
Sculptor, preferably:
Marble, granite, bronze.
Durable.
Something nice with swans
That's durable
Forever.
All it has to be is good.
(Looking over GEORGE's shoulder at his work, then at GEORGE)
And George, you're good.
You're really good.

George's stroke is tender,
George's touch is pure.
(Sits or stands nearby and watches him intently)
Your eyes, George.
I love your eyes, George.

31

I love your beard, George.
I love your size, George.
But most, George,
Of all,
But most of all,
I love your painting . . .
                    (*Looking up at the sun*)
I think I'm fainting . . .
    (*Steps back into dress, resumes pose, gives a twitch and
    a wince, then sings sotto voce again*)
The tip of a stay.
                    (*Wince*)
Right under the tit.
No, don't give in, just
                    (*Shifts*)   .
Lift the arm a bit . . .

GEORGE

Don't lift the arm, please.

DOT

Sunday in the park with George . . .

GEORGE

The bustle high, please.

DOT

Not even a nod.
As if I were trees.
The ground could open,
He would still say "please."

Never know with you, George,
Who could know with you?

32

The others I knew, George.
Before we get through,
I'll get to you, too.

God, I am so hot!

Well, there are worse things
Than staring at the water on a Sunday.
There are worse things
Than staring at the water
As you're posing for a picture
After sleeping on the ferry
After getting up at seven
To come over to an island
In the middle of a river
Half an hour from the city
On a Sunday.
On a Sunday in the park with —

GEORGE
(*The music stopping*)

Don't move the mouth!!

DOT
(*Holds absolutely still for a very long beat. As music resumes, SHE pours all her extremely mixed emotions into one word*)
— George!

I am getting tired. The sun is too strong today.

GEORGE

Almost finished.

DOT
(*Sexy*)
I'd rather be in the studio, George.

GEORGE
(*Wryly*)
I know.

OLD LADY
(*Looking across the water*)
They are out early today.

NURSE
It is Sunday, Madame.

OLD LADY
That is what I mean, Nurse! Young boys out swimming so early on a Sunday?

NURSE
Well, it is very warm.

OLD LADY
Hand me my parasol.

NURSE
I am, Madame.
(NURSE *stands up and opens the parasol for the* OLD LADY. FRANZ, *a coachman, enters; stares at the* TWO WOMEN *for a moment.* HE *sees* GEORGE, *and affects a pose as* HE *sits*)

DOT
Oh, no.

GEORGE

What?

DOT

Look. Look who is over there.

GEORGE

So?

DOT

When he is around, you know who is likely to follow.

GEORGE

You have moved your arm.

DOT

I think they are spying on you, George. I really do.

GEORGE

Are you going to hold your head still?
(*The* NURSE *has wandered over in the vicinity of* FRANZ)

NURSE

You are here awfully early today.

FRANZ

(*Speaks with a German accent*)
Ja. So are you.

NURSE

And working on a Sunday.

FRANZ

Ja . . .

35

NURSE

It is a beautiful day.

FRANZ
(*Sexy*)

It is too hot.

NURSE

Do you think?

OLD LADY

Where is my fan!

NURSE

I have to go back.

OLD LADY

Nurse, my fan!

NURSE

You did not bring it today, Madame.

OLD LADY

Of course I brought it!

FRANZ

Perhaps we will see each other later.

NURSE

Perhaps . . .

OLD LADY

There it is. Over there.

36

(OLD LADY *picks up the fan*)

NURSE

That is my fan —

OLD LADY

Well, I can use it. Can I not? It was just lying there . . . What is all that commotion?
>(*Music. Laughter from off right. A wagon tracks on bearing a tableau vivant of Seurat's "Une Baignade Asnières"*)

FRANZ

Jungen! Nicht so laut! Ruhe, bitte!
>(*The following is heard simultaneously from the characters in the tableau*)

BOY

Yoo-hoo! Dumb and fat!

YOUNG MAN

Hey! Who you staring at?

MAN

Look at the lady with the rear!
>(*The* YOUNG MAN *gives a loud Bronx cheer*)

BOY

Yoo-hoo — kinky beard!

MAN

Kinky beard.

Kinky beard!

(GEORGE *gestures, as when an artist raises and ex-tends his right arm to frame an image before him —* ALL *freeze. Silence. A frame comes in around them.* JULES *and* YVONNE, *a well-to-do middle-aged couple, stroll on and pause before the painting*)

JULES

Ahh . . .

YVONNE

Ooh . . .

JULES

Mmm . . .

YVONNE

Oh, dear.

JULES

Oh, my.

YVONNE

Oh, my dear.

JULES
(*Sings*)

It has no presence.

YVONNE
(*Sings*)

No passion.

38

                    JULES
No life.

                    (THEY *laugh*)

It's neither pastoral
Nor lyrical.

                    YVONNE
                    (*Giggling*)
You don't suppose that it's satirical?
                    (THEY *laugh heartily*)

                    JULES
Just density
Without intensity —

                    YVONNE
No life.

Boys with their clothes off —

                    JULES
                    (*Mocking*)
I must paint a factory next!

                    YVONNE
It's so mechanical.

                    JULES
Methodical.

                    YVONNE
It might be in some dreary
Socialistic periodical.

                    39

JULES
(*Approvingly*)

Good.

YVONNE

So drab, so cold.

JULES

And so controlled.

BOTH

No life.

JULES

His touch is too deliberate, somehow.

YVONNE

The dog.

(THEY *shriek with laughter*)

JULES

These things get hung —

YVONNE

Hmm.

JULES

And then they're gone.

YVONNE

Ahhh . . .

Of course he's young —

(JULES *shoots her a look. Hastily*)
But getting on.

                         JULES
Oh . . .

All mind, no heart.
No life in his art.

                        YVONNE
No life in his *life* —
                    (JULES *nods in approval*)

                         BOTH
No —
                (THEY *giggle and chortle*)
Life.
    (*Arpeggio. The* BOYS *in the picture give a loud Bronx
    cheer.* JULES *and* YVONNE *turn and slowly stroll up-
    stage, as the tableau disappears*)

                        NURSE
                (*Seeing* JULES)
There is that famous artist — what is his name . . .

                      OLD LADY
What *is* his name?

                        NURSE
I can never remember their names.
    (JULES *tips his hat to the* LADIES. *The* COUPLE *contin-
    ues towards* GEORGE)

                          41

JULES

George! Out very early today.
> (GEORGE *nods as* HE *continues sketching.* DOT *turns her back on them*)

GEORGE

Hello, Jules.

YVONNE

A lovely day . . .

JULES

I couldn't be out sketching today — it is too sunny!
> (YVONNE *laughs*)

GEORGE

Have you seen the painting?

JULES

Yes. I was just going to say! Boys bathing — what a curious subject.
> (YVONNE *stops him*)

We must speak.

YVONNE
> (*Sincere*)

I loved the dog.
> (*Beat*)

JULES

I *am* pleased there was an independent exhibition.

GEORGE

Yes . . .

JULES

We *must* speak. Really.

YVONNE

Enjoy the weather.

JULES

Good day.
(*As* THEY *exit,* YVONNE *stops* JULES *and points to* DOT)

YVONNE

That dress!
(SHE *laughs, and* THEY *exit*)

DOT

I hate them!

GEORGE

Jules is a fine painter.

DOT

I do not care. I hate them.
(JULES *and* YVONNE *return*)

JULES

Franz!

YVONNE

We are waiting!
(THEY *exit*)

FRANZ

Ja, Madame, Monsieur. At your service.
(FRANZ, *who has been hiding behind a tree, eyeing the*

43

NURSE, *quickly dashes offstage after* JULES *and* YVONNE.
GEORGE *closes his pad.* DOT *remains frozen*)

GEORGE

Thank you.

(*Beat*)

DOT
(*Moving*)

I began to do it.

GEORGE

What?

DOT

Concentrate. Like you said.

GEORGE
(*Patronizing*)

You did very well.

DOT

Did I really?

GEORGE
(*Gathering his belongings*)

Yes. I'll meet you back at the studio.

DOT
(*Annoyed*)

You are not coming?

GEORGE

Not now.

44

(*Angry,* DOT *begins to exit*)

Dot. We'll go to the Follies tonight.

    (SHE *stops, looks at him, then walks off.* GEORGE *walks*
    to the NURSE *and* OLD LADY)

Bon jour.

NURSE

Bon jour, Monsieur.

GEORGE

Lovely morning, Ladies.

NURSE

Yes.

GEORGE

I have my pad and crayons today.

NURSE

Oh, that would —

OLD LADY

Not today!

GEORGE
(*Disappointed*)

Why not today?

OLD LADY

Too warm.

GEORGE

It *is* warm, but it will not take long. You can go —

45

OLD LADY
(*Continues to look out across the water*)
Some other day, Monsieur.
(*Beat*)

GEORGE
(*Kneeling*)
It's George, Mother.

OLD LADY
(*As if it is to be a secret*)
Sssh . . .

GEORGE
(*Getting up*)
Yes. I guess we will all be back.
(HE *exits as lights fade to black*)

(GEORGE's *studio. Downstage,* DOT [*in a likeness of Seurat's "La Poudreuse"*] *is at her vanity, powdering her face. Steady, unhurried, persistent rhythmic figure underneath*)

DOT
(*As* SHE *powders rhythmically*)
George taught me all about concentration. "The art of being still," he said.
(*Checks herself, then resumes powdering*)
I guess I did not learn it soon enough.
(*Dips puff in powder*)
George likes to be alone.
(*Resumes powdering*)

46

Sometimes he will work all night long painting. We fought about that. I need sleep. I love to dream.

(*Upstage,* GEORGE *on a scaffold, behind a large canvas, which is a scrim, comes into view.* HE *is painting. It is an in-progress version of the painting "A Sunday Afternoon on the Island of La Grande Jatte"*)

George doesn't need as much sleep as everyone else.

(*Dips puff, starts powdering neck*)

And he never tells me his dreams. George has many secrets.

(*Lights down on* DOT, *up on* GEORGE. *A number of brushes in his hand,* HE *is covering a section of the canvas — the face of the woman in the foreground — with tiny specks of paint, in the same rhythm as* DOT's *powdering*)

GEORGE
(*Pauses, checks*)

Order.

(*Dabs with another color, pauses, checks, dabs palette*)

Design.

(*Dabs with another brush*)

Composition.
Tone.
Form.
Symmetry.
Balance.

(*Sings*)

More red . . .

(*Dabs with more intensity*)

And a little more red . . .

(*Switches brushes*)

Blue blue blue blue

47

Blue blue blue blue
Even even . . .

> (*Switches quickly*)

Good . . .

> (*Humming*)

Bumbum bum bumbumbum
Bumbum bum . . .

> (*Paints silently for a moment*)

More red . . .

> (*Switches brushes again*)

More blue . . .

> (*Again*)

More beer . . .

(*Takes a swig from a nearby bottle, always eyeing the canvas, puts the bottle down*)

More light!

(HE *dabs assiduously, delicately attacking the area* HE *is painting*)

Color and light.
There's only color and light.
Yellow and white.
Just blue and yellow and white.

> (*Addressing the woman* HE *is painting*)

Look at the air, Miss —

> (*Dabs at the space in front of her*)

See what I mean?
No, look over there, Miss —

> (*Dabs at her eye, pauses, checks it*)

That's done with green . . .

> (*Swirling a brush in the orange cup*)

Conjoined with orange . . .

(*Lights down on* GEORGE, *up on* DOT, *now powdering her breasts and armpits. Rhythmic figure persists underneath*)

Nothing seems to fit me right.
> (*Giggles*)

The less I wear, the more comfortable I feel.
> (*Sings, checking herself*)

More rouge . . .
> (*Puts puff down, gets rouge, starts applying it in small rhythmic circles, speaks*)

George is very special. Maybe I'm just not special enough for him.
> (*Puts rouge down, picks up eyebrow tweezers, sings*)

If my legs were longer.
> (*Plucks at her eyebrow*)

If my bust was smaller.
> (*Plucks*)

If my hands were graceful.
> (*Plucks*)

If my waist was thinner.
> (*Checks herself*)

If my hips were flatter.
> (*Plucks again*)

If my voice was warm.
> (*Plucks*)

If I could concentrate —
> (*Abruptly, her feet start to can-can under the table*)

I'd be in the Follies.
I'd be in a cabaret.
Gentlemen in tall silk hats
And linen spats
Would wait with flowers.
I could make them wait for hours.
Giddy young aristocrats
With fancy flats
Who'd drink my health,

49

And I would be as
Hard as nails . . .
     (Looks at her nails, reaches for the buffer)
And they'd only want me more . . .
       (Starts buffing nails rhythmically)
If I was a Folly girl.
Nah, I wouldn't like it much.
Married men and stupid boys
And too much smoke and all that noise
And all that color and light . . .
    (Lights up on GEORGE, *talking to the woman in the painting. Rhythmic figure continues underneath)*

GEORGE

Aren't you proper today, Miss? Your parasol so properly cocked, your bustle so perfectly upright. No doubt your chin rests at just the proper angle from your chest.
    (Addressing the figure of the man next to her)
And you, Sir. Your hat so black. So black to you, perhaps. So red to me.
    (The rhythmic figure drops out momentarily)

DOT
(Spraying herself with perfume)
None of the others worked at night . . .

GEORGE

So composed for a Sunday.

DOT

How do you work without the right
        (Sprays)
Bright

(*Sprays*)

White

(*Sprays*)

Light?

(*Sprays*)

How do you fathom George?

(*Rhythmic figure returns underneath*)

(*Muttering, trancelike, as* HE *paints*)

Red red red red
Red red orange
Red red orange
Orange pick up blue
Pick up red
Pick up orange
From the blue-green blue-green
Blue-green circle
On the violet diagonal
Di-ag-ag-ag-ag-ag-o-nal-nal
Yellow comma yellow comma

(*Humming, massaging his numb wrist*)

Numnum num numnumnum
Numnum num . . .

(*Sniffs, smelling* DOT's *perfume*)

Blue blue blue blue
Blue still sitting
Red that perfume
Blue all night
Blue-green the window shut
Dut dut dut
Dot Dot sitting
Dot Dot waiting

51

Dot Dot getting fat fat fat
More yellow
Dot Dot waiting to go
Out out out but
No no no George
Finish the hat finish the hat
Have to finish the hat first
Hat hat hat hat
Hot hot hot it's hot in here . . .
                    (*Whistles a bit, then joyfully*)
Sunday!

Color and light!

                         DOT
                 (*Pinning up her hair*)
But how George looks. He could look forever.

                      GEORGE
There's only color and light.

                         DOT
As if he sees you and he doesn't all at once.

                      GEORGE
Purple and white . . .

                         DOT
What is he thinking when he looks like that?

                      GEORGE
. . . And red and purple and white.

                          52

What does he see? Sometimes, not even blinking.

(*To the young girls in the painting*)
Look at this glade, girls,
Your cool blue spot.

DOT

His eyes. So dark and shiny.

GEORGE

No, stay in the shade, girls.
It's getting hot . . .

DOT

Some think cold and black.

GEORGE

It's getting orange . . .

DOT
(*Sings*)
But it's warm inside his eyes . . .

GEORGE
(*Dabbing more intensely*)
Hotter . . .

DOT

And it's soft inside his eyes . . .
(GEORGE *steps around the canvas to get paint or clean*

53

a brush. HE *glances at* DOT. *Their eyes meet for a second, then* DOT *turns back to her mirror*)
And he burns you with his eyes . . .

GEORGE

Look at her looking.

DOT

And you're studied like the light.

GEORGE

Forever with that mirror. What does she see? The round face, the tiny pout, the soft mouth, the creamy skin . . .

DOT

And you look inside the eyes.

GEORGE

The pink lips, the red cheeks . . .

DOT

And you catch him here and there.

GEORGE

The wide eyes. Studying the round face, the tiny pout . . .

DOT

But he's never really there.

GEORGE

Seeing all the parts and none of the whole.

DOT

So you want him even more.

GEORGE
(*Sings*)

But the way she catches light . . .

DOT

And you drown inside his eyes . . .

GEORGE

And the color of her hair . . .

GEORGE	DOT
I could look at her	I could look at him
Forever . . .	Forever . . .

　　　(A *long beat. Music holds under, gradually fading*)

GEORGE
(*At his work table*)

It's going well . . .

DOT

Should I wear my red dress or blue?

GEORGE

Red.

(*Beat*)

DOT

Aren't you going to clean up?

55

GEORGE

Why?

DOT

The Follies, George!

(*Beat*)

GEORGE

I have to finish the hat.

(HE *returns to his work.* DOT *slams down her brush and stares at the back of the canvas.* SHE *exits. Lights fade downstage as the rhythmic figure resumes. As* HE *paints*)

Damn. The Follies. Will she yell or stay silent? Go without me or sulk in the corner? Will she be in the bed when the hat and the grass and the parasol have finally found their way? . . .

(*Sings*)

Too green . . .

Do I care? . . .

Too blue . . .

Yes . . .

Too soft . . .

What shall I do?

(*Thinks for a moment*)

Well . . .

Red.

(*Continues painting; music swells as* HE *is consumed by light*)

(*Afternoon. Another Sunday on the island. Downstage right* GEORGE *sketches a* BOATMAN; *a cut-out of a black* DOG *stands close by;* NURSE *and* OLD LADY *sit near their tree.* CELESTE #1 *and* CELESTE #2, *young shopgirls, sit on a bench stage left*)

56

BOATMAN

The water looks different on Sunday.

GEORGE

It is the same water you boat on all week.

BOATMAN
(*Contentious*)

It looks different from the park.

GEORGE

You prefer watching the boats to the people promenading?

BOATMAN
(*Laughing*)

People all dressed up in their Sunday-best pretending? Sunday is just another day.

> (DOT *and* LOUIS *enter arm in arm.* THEY *look out at the water*)

I wear what I always wear — then I don't have to worry.

GEORGE

Worry?

BOATMAN

They leave me alone dressed like this. No one comes near.
> (*Music under*)

CELESTE #1

Look who's over there.

CELESTE #2

Dot! Who is she with?

CELESTE #1

Looks like Louis the baker.

CELESTE #2

How did Dot get to be with Louis?

CELESTE #1

She knows how to make dough rise!
                    (THEY *laugh*)

NURSE
(*Noticing* DOT)

There is that woman.

OLD LADY

Who is she with?

NURSE
(*Squinting*)

Looks like the baker.

OLD LADY

Moving up, I suppose.

NURSE

The artist is more handsome.
                    (DOT *and* LOUIS *exit*)

OLD LADY

You cannot eat paintings, my dear — not when there's bread in
the oven.
        (JULES, YVONNE, *and their child* LOUISE *appear.* THEY
        *stand to one side and strike a pose. Music continues
        under, slow and stately*)

58

JULES

They say he is working on an enormous canvas.

YVONNE

I heard somewhere he's painting little specks.

JULES

You heard it from me! A large canvas of specks. Really . . .

YVONNE

Look at him. Drawing a slovenly boatman.

JULES

I think he is trying to play with light.

YVONNE

What next?

JULES

A monkey cage, they say.

(THEY *laugh*)

BOATMAN

Sunday hypocrites. That's what they are. Muttering and murmuring about this one and that one. I'll take my old dog for company any day. A dog knows his place. Respects your privacy. Makes no demands.

(*To the* DOG)

Right, Spot?

SPOT (GEORGE)

Right.

CELESTE #1
(*Sings*)
They say that George has another woman.

CELESTE #2
(*Sings*)
I'm not surprised.

CELESTE #1
They say that George only lives with tramps.

CELESTE #2
I'm not surprised.

CELESTE #1
They say he prowls through the streets
In his top hat after midnight —

CELESTE #2
No!

CELESTE #1
— and stands there staring up at the lamps.

CELESTE #2
I'm not surprised.

BOTH
Artists are so crazy . . .

OLD LADY
Those girls are noisy.

60

NURSE

Yes, Madame.

OLD LADY
(*Referring to* JULES)

That man is famous.

NURSE

Yes, Madame.

OLD LADY
(*Referring to* BOATMAN)

That man is filthy.

NURSE

Your son seems to find him interesting.

OLD LADY

That man's deluded.

(NURSE *thinks, nods*)

THE CELESTES

Artists are so crazy.

OLD LADY *and* NURSE

Artists are so peculiar.

YVONNE

Monkeys!

BOATMAN

Overprivileged women
Complaining,

61

Silly little simpering
Shopgirls,
Condescending artists
"Observing,"
"Perceiving" . . .
Well, screw them!

ALL

Artists are so —

CELESTE #2

Crazy.

CELESTE #1

Secretive.

BOATMAN

High and mighty.

NURSE

Interesting.

OLD LADY

Unfeeling.

BOATMAN

What do you do with those drawings, anyway?
(DOT *and* LOUIS *re-enter*)

DOT
(*To* LOUIS)

That's George.
(ALL *heads turn, first to* DOT, *then to* GEORGE)

JULES

There's a move on to include his work in the next group show.

YVONNE

Never!

JULES

I agree.

(*Pause*)

I agree.

(THEY *exit. Music stops*)

CELESTE #1

He draws anyone.

CELESTE #2

Old boatman!

CELESTE #1

Peculiar man.

CELESTE #2

Like his father, I said.

CELESTE #1

I said so first.

(LOUIS *escorts* DOT *to a park bench stage left and exits.*
SHE *sits with a small red lesson book in hand*)

DOT

(*Very slowly,* SHE *reads aloud*)

"Lesson number eight. Pro-nouns."

(*Proudly,* SHE *repeats the word, looking towards*
GEORGE)
Pronouns.

(SHE *reads*)
"What is a pronoun? A pronoun is the word used in the place
of a noun. Do you recall what a noun is?"

(*Looks up*)
Certainly, I recall.

(SHE *pauses, then quickly flips back in the book to the
earlier lesson on nouns.* SHE *nods her head knowingly,
then flips back to the present lesson.* SHE *reads*)
"Example: Charles has a book. Marie wants Charles' book."

(*To herself*)
Not Marie again . . .

(*Reads*)
"Marie wants *his* book. Fill in the blanks. Charles ran with Marie's ball. Charles ran with . . .

(SHE *writes as* SHE *spells aloud*)
h – e – r ball."

(*To herself*)
Get the ball back, Marie.

(LOUISE *dashes in upstage*)

OLD LADY

Children should not go unattended.

NURSE

She is very young to be alone.

OLD LADY

I do not like what I see today, Nurse.

64

NURSE
(*Confused*)

What do you see?

OLD LADY

Lack of discipline.

NURSE

Oh.

OLD LADY

Not the right direction at all.

BOATMAN

Fools rowing. Call that recreation!

GEORGE

Almost finished.
>   (LOUISE *has come up to pet the dog.* BOATMAN *turns
>   on her in a fury*)

BOATMAN

Get away from that dog!
>   (ALL *eyes turn to the* BOATMAN. LOUISE *screams and
>   goes running offstage crying.*)

GEORGE

That was hardly necessary!

BOATMAN

How do you know what's necessary? Who are you, with your
fancy pad and crayons? You call that work? You smug goddam

holier-than-thou shitty little men in your fancy clothes — born
with pens and pencils, not pricks! You don't know . . .

    (BOATMAN *storms off.* GEORGE, *stunned, begins to draw
the dog*)

CELESTE #1
(*To* GEORGE)

Well, what are you going to do — now that you have no one to
draw?

CELESTE #2

Sshh. Don't talk to him.

GEORGE

I am drawing his dog.

CELESTE #2

His dog!

CELESTE #1

Honestly . . .

GEORGE

I have already sketched you ladies.

CELESTE #1

What!

CELESTE #2

You have?

    (*The* CELESTES *approach* GEORGE)

CELESTE #1

I do not believe you.

CELESTE #2

When?
>   (*During the above, the* OLD LADY *and* NURSE *have ex-
>   ited*)

GEORGE

A few Sundays ago.

CELESTE #1

But we never sat for you.

GEORGE

I studied you from afar.

CELESTE #2

No!

CELESTE #1

Where were you?

CELESTE #2

I want to see.

GEORGE

Some day you shall.

THE CELESTES

When?

67

GEORGE

Good day.

(GEORGE *moves upstage*)

CELESTE #1

He did not so much as ask.

CELESTE #2

No respect for a person's privacy.

CELESTE #1

I would not sit for him anyway.

CELESTE #2

Probably that's why he did not ask.

(THEY *exit*)

GEORGE

(*From across the stage to* DOT)

Good afternoon.

DOT

(*Surprised*)

Hello.

GEORGE

Lesson number eight?

DOT

Yes. Pronouns. My writing is improving. I even keep notes in the back of the book.

Good for you.

DOT

How is your painting coming along?

GEORGE

Slowly.

DOT

Are you getting more work done now that you have fewer distractions in the studio?

GEORGE
(*Beat;* HE *moves closer*)
It has been quiet there.
(LOUIS *bounds onstage with a pastry tin*)

LOUIS

Dot. I made your favorite —
(HE *stops when* HE *sees* GEORGE)

GEORGE

Good day.
(HE *retreats across the stage.* DOT *watches him, then turns to* LOUIS)

LOUIS
(*Opens the tin*)
Creampuffs!
(*The bench on which* THEY *are sitting tracks offstage as* DOT *continues to look at* GEORGE. GEORGE, *who has*

69

been staring at his sketch of SPOT, *looks over and sees*
THEY *have left. Music. Lights change, leaving the dog*
onstage. GEORGE *sketches the dog*)

GEORGE
(*Sings*)

If the head was smaller.
If the tail were longer.
If he faced the water.
If the paws were hidden.
If the neck was darker.
If the back was curved.
More like the parasol.

Bumbum bum bumbumbum
Bumbum bum . . .

More shade.
More tail.

More grass . . .
Would you like some more grass?
Mmmm . . .

SPOT (GEORGE)
(*Barks*)

Ruff! Ruff!
Thanks, the week has been
(*Barks*)
Rough!
When you're stuck for life on a garbage scow —
(*Sniffs around*)

70

Only forty feet long from stern to prow,
And a crackpot in the bow — wow, rough!
                    (*Sniffs*)

The planks are rough
And the wind is rough
And the master's drunk and mean and —
                    (*Sniffs*)

Grrrruff! Gruff!
With the fish and scum
And planks and ballast —
                    (*Sniffs*)

The nose gets numb
And the paws get calloused.
And with splinters in your ass,
You look forward to the grass
On Sunday.
The day off.
                    (*Barks*)

Off! Off! Off!
Off!

The grass needs to be thicker. Perhaps a few weeds. With some
ants, if you would. I love fresh ants.

Roaming around on Sunday,
Poking among the roots and rocks.
Nose to the ground on Sunday,
Studying all the shoes and socks.
Everything's worth it Sunday,
The day off.
                    (*Sniffs*)

Bits of pastry.
                    (*Sniffs*)

71

Piece of chicken.
                    (*Sniffs*)
Here's a handkerchief
That somebody was sick in.
                    (*Sniffs*)
There's a thistle.
                    (*Sniffs*)
That's a shallot.
                    (*Sniffs*)
That's a dripping
From the loony with the palette.
          (A *cut-out of a pug dog*, FIFI, *appears*)

                    FIFI (GEORGE)
Yap! Yap!
                    (*Pants*)
Yap!

Out for the day on Sunday,
Off of my lady's lap at last.
Yapping away on Sunday
Helps you forget the week just past —
                    (*Yelps*)
Yep! Yep!
Everything's worth it Sunday,
The day off.
Yep!
Stuck all week on a lady's lap,
Nothing to do but yawn and nap,
Can you blame me if I yap?

                    SPOT
Nope.

72

FIFI

There's just so much attention a dog can take.

Being alone on Sunday,
Rolling around in mud and dirt —

SPOT

Begging a bone on Sunday,
Settling for a spoiled dessert —

FIFI

Everything's worth it

SPOT

Sunday —

FIFI

The day off.

SPOT
(*Sniffs*)

Something fuzzy.

FIFI
(*Sniffs*)

Something furry.

SPOT
(*Sniffs*)

Something pink
That someone tore off in a hurry.

FIFI

What's the muddle
In the middle?

73

That's the puddle
Where the poodle did the piddle.
> (HORN PLAYER *rises from the stage. Two horn calls.*
> *Music continues under. Enter* FRANZ; FRIEDA, *his wife;*
> *the* CELESTES, *with fishing poles; and* NURSE)

GEORGE

Taking the day on Sunday,
Now that the dreary week is dead.
Getting away on Sunday
Brightens the dreary week ahead.
Everyone's on display on Sunday —

ALL

The day off!
> (GEORGE *flips open a page of his sketchbook and starts*
> *to sketch the* NURSE *as* SHE *clucks at the ducks*)

GEORGE

Bonnet flapping,
Bustle sliding,
Like a rocking horse that nobody's been riding.
There's a daisy —
And some clover —
And that interesting fellow looking over . . .

OLD LADY
(*Offstage*)

Nurse!

NURSE *and* GEORGE

One day is much like any other,
Listening to her snap and drone.

74

NURSE

Still, Sunday with someone's dotty mother
Is better than Sunday with your own.
Mothers may drone, mothers may whine —
Tending to his, though, is perfectly fine.
It pays for the nurse that is tending to mine
On Sunday,
My day off.

(*The* CELESTES, *fishing. Music continues under*)

CELESTE #2

This is just ridiculous.

CELESTE #1

Why shouldn't we fish.

CELESTE #2

No one will notice us anyway.

(SOLDIER *enters, attached to a life-size cut-out of another soldier, his* COMPANION)

CELESTE #1

Look.

CELESTE #2

Where?

CELESTE #1

Soldiers.

CELESTE #2

Alone.

CELESTE #1

What did I tell you?

75

CELESTE #2

They'll never talk to us if we fish. Why don't we —

CELESTE #1

It's a beautiful day for fishing.
> (SHE *smiles in the direction of the* SOLDIERS)

SOLDIER
> (*Looking to his* COMPANION)

What do you think?
> (*Beat*)

I like the one in the light hat.
> (LOUISE *enters, notices* FRIEDA *and* FRANZ, *and dashes over to them*)

LOUISE

Frieda, Frieda —

FRANZ

Oh, no.

FRIEDA
> (*Speaks with a German accent*)

Not now, Louise.

LOUISE

I want to play.

FRANZ

Go away, Louise. We are not working today.

LOUISE

Let's go throw stones at the ducks.

FRIEDA

Louise! Do not throw stones at the ducks!

LOUISE

Why not?

FRANZ

You know why not, and you know this is our day off, so go find
your mother and throw some stones at her, why don't you.
(HE *begins to choke* LOUISE; FRIEDA *releases his grip*)

FRIEDA

Franz!

LOUISE

I'm telling.

FRANZ

Good. Go!
(LOUISE *exits*)

FRIEDA

Franzel — relax.

FRANZ

Ja . . . relax.
(*He opens a bottle of wine.* GEORGE *flips a page and
starts to sketch* FRANZ *and* FRIEDA)

GEORGE *and* FRIEDA

Second bottle . . .

77

GEORGE *and* FRANZ
(As FRANZ *looks off at* NURSE)

Ah, she looks for me . . .

FRIEDA

He is bursting to go . . .

FRANZ

Near the fountain . . .

FRIEDA

I could let him . . .

FRANZ

How to manage it — ?

FRIEDA

No.

You know, Franz — I believe that artist is drawing us.

FRANZ

Who?

FRIEDA

Monsieur's friend.

FRANZ
(*Sees* GEORGE. THEY *pose*)

Monsieur would never think to draw us! We are only people he looks down upon.
(*Pause*)
I should have been an artist. I was never intended for work.

Artists work, Franz. I believe they work very hard.

Work! . . . *We* work.

(*Sings*)

We serve their food,
We carve their meat,
We tend to their house,
We polish their
Silverware.

The food we serve
We also eat.

For them we rush,
Wash and brush,
Wipe and wax —

Franz, relax.

While he "creates,"
We scrape their plates
And dust their knickknacks,
Hundreds to the shelf.
Work is what you do for others,
Liebchen,
Art is what you do for yourself.

79

(JULES *enters, as if looking for someone. Notices* GEORGE *instead*)

JULES

Working on Sunday again? You should give yourself a day off.

GEORGE

Why?

JULES

You must need time to replenish — or does your well never run dry?
(*Laughs; notices* FRIEDA *and* FRANZ)
Drawing my servants? Certainly, George, you could find more colorful subjects.

GEORGE

Who should I be sketching?

JULES

How about that pretty friend of yours. Now why did I see her arm-in-arm with the baker today?
(GEORGE *looks up*)
She is a pretty subject.

GEORGE

Yes . . .
(BOATMAN *enters*)

JULES

Your life needs spice, George. Go to some parties. That is where you'll meet prospective buyers. Have some fun. The work is bound to reflect —

80

GEORGE

You don't like my work, do you?

JULES

I did once.

GEORGE

You find it too tight.

JULES

People are talking about your work. You have your admirers, but you —

GEORGE

I am using a different brushstroke.

JULES
(*Getting angry*)
Always changing! Why keep changing?

GEORGE

Because I do not paint for your approval.
(*Beat*)

JULES

And I suppose that is why I like you.
(*Begins to walk away*)
Good to see you, George.
(JULES *crosses as if to exit*)

GEORGE
(*Calling after him*)
Jules! I would like you to come to the studio some time. See the new work . . .

81

JULES

For my approval?

GEORGE

No! For your opinion.

JULES
(*Considers the offer*)
Very well.
(HE *exits.* GEORGE *flips a page over and starts sketching the* BOATMAN)

GEORGE *and* BOATMAN

You and me, pal,
We're the loonies.
Did you know that?
Bet you didn't know that.

BOATMAN

'Cause we tell them the truth.

Who you drawing?
Who the hell you think you're drawing?
Me?
You don't know me!
Go on drawing,
Since you're drawing only what you want to see,
Anyway!
(*Points to his eyepatch*)
One eye, no illusion —
That you get with two:
(*Points to* GEORGE's *eye*)

One for what is true.
                    (*Points to the other*)
One for what suits you.
Draw your wrong conclusion,
All you artists do.
I see what is true . . .
                    (*Music continues under*)
Sitting there, looking everyone up and down. Studying every
move like *you* see something different, like your eyes know
more —

You and me, pal,
We're society's fault.
          (YVONNE, LOUISE, OLD LADY *enter.* GEORGE *packs up
          his belongings*)

ALL

Taking the day on Sunday
After another week is dead.

OLD LADY

Nurse!

ALL

Getting away on Sunday
Brightens the dreary week ahead.

OLD LADY

Nurse!
          (GEORGE *begins to exit, crossing paths with* DOT *and*
          LOUIS, *who enter.* HE *gives* DOT *a hasty tip-of-the-hat
          and makes a speedy exit*)

83

Leaving the city pressure
Behind you,
Off where the air is fresher,
Where green, blue,
Blind you —
> (LOUIS *leaves* DOT *to offer some pastries to his friends in the park. Throughout the song,* HE *divides his time between* DOT *and the others*)

DOT
> (*Looking offstage in the direction of* GEORGE's *exit*)

Hello, George . . .
Where did you go, George?
I know you're near, George.
I caught your eyes, George.
I want your ear, George.
I've a surprise, George . . .

Everybody loves Louis,
Louis' simple and kind.
Everybody loves Louis,
Louis' lovable.

FRANZ
Louis!

DOT
Seems we never know, do we,
Who we're going to find?
> (*Tenderly*)

And Louis the baker is not what I had in mind.
But . . .

Louis' really an artist:
Louis' cakes are an art.
Louis isn't the smartest —
Louis' popular.
Everybody loves Louis:
Louis bakes from the heart . . .

The bread, George.
I mean the bread, George.
And then in bed, George . . .
I mean he kneads me —
I mean like dough, George . . .
Hello, George . . .

Louis' always so pleasant,
Louis' always so fair.
Louis makes you feel present,
Louis' generous.
That's the thing about Louis:
Louis always is "there."
Louis' thoughts are not hard to follow,
Louis' art is not hard to swallow.

Not that Louis' perfection —
That's what makes him ideal.
Hardly anything worth objection:
Louis drinks a bit,
Louis blinks a bit.
Louis makes a connection,
That's the thing that you feel . . .

We lose things.
And then we choose things.

And there are Louis's
And there are Georges —
Well, Louis's
And George.

But George has George
And I need —
Someone —
Louis — !

> (LOUIS *gives her a pastry and exits*)

Everybody loves Louis,
Him as well as his cakes.
Everybody loves Louis,
Me included, George.
Not afraid to be gooey,
Louis sells what he makes.
Everybody gets along with him.
That's the trouble, nothing's wrong with him.

Louis has to bake his way,
George can only bake his . . .

> (*Licks a pastry*)

Louis it is!

> (SHE *throws pastry away and exits. Enter an American southern couple,* MR. *and* MRS., *followed by* GEORGE, *who sketches them.* THEY *are overdressed, eating French pastries and studying the people in the park*)

MR.

Paris looks nothin' like the paintings.

MRS.

I know.

MR.

(*Looking about*)

I don't see any passion, do you?

MRS.

None.

MR.

The French are so placid.

MRS.

I don't think they have much style, either.

MR.

What's all the carryin' on back home? Delicious pastries, though.

MRS.

Excellent.

MR.

Lookin' at those boats over there makes me think of our return voyage.

MRS.

I long to be back home.

MR.

You do?

MRS.

How soon could we leave?

MR.

You're that anxious to leave? But, Peaches, we just arrived!

I know!

MR.
(*Gives it a moment's thought*)
I don't like it here either! We'll go right back to the hotel and I'll book passage for the end of the week. We'll go to the galleries this afternoon and then we'll be on our way home!

MRS.

I am so relieved.
(As THEY *exit*)
I *will* miss these pastries, though.

MR.

We'll take a baker with us, too.

MRS.

Wonderful!
(THEY *exit*)

CELESTE # 1
You really should try using that pole.

CELESTE #2
It won't make any difference.

CELESTE #1
(*Starts yelping as if* SHE *had caught a fish*)
Oh! Oh!

CELESTE #2
What is wrong?

CELESTE #1
Just sit there.

(SHE *carries on some more, looking in the direction of the* SOLDIER *and his* COMPANION, *who converse for a moment, then come over*)

SOLDIER

May we be of some service, Madame?

CELESTE #1

Mademoiselle.

CELESTE #2

She has a fish.

CELESTE #1

He knows.

SOLDIER

Allow me.
(SOLDIER *takes the pole from her and pulls in the line and hook. There is nothing on the end*)

CELESTE #1

Oh. It tugged so . . .

SOLDIER

There's no sign of a fish here.

CELESTE #1

Oh me. My name is Celeste. This is my friend.

CELESTE #2

Celeste.
(SOLDIER *fools with fishing pole*)

CELESTE #1

Do you have a name?

SOLDIER

I beg your pardon. Napoleon. Some people feel I should change it.

(*The* CELESTES *shake their heads no*)

CELESTE #2

And your friend?

SOLDIER

Yes. He is my friend.

CELESTE #1
(*Giggling, to* SOLDIER)

He's very quiet.

SOLDIER

Yes. Actually he is. He lost his hearing during combat exercises.

CELESTE #1

What a shame.

SOLDIER

He can't speak, either.

CELESTE #2

Oh. How dreadful.

SOLDIER

We have become very close, though.

CELESTE #1
(*Nervous*)

So I see.

(*Music*)

90

SOLDIER *and* GEORGE
(*Sudden and loud*)

Mademoiselles,
I and my friend,
We are but soldiers!
(*Rumble from his* COMPANION: SOLDIER *raises hand to quiet him*)

SOLDIER

Passing the time
In between wars
For weeks at an end.

CELESTE #1
(*Aside*)

Both of them are perfect.

CELESTE #2

You can have the other.

CELESTE #1

I don't want the other.

CELESTE #2

I don't want the other either.

SOLDIER

And after a week
Spent mostly indoors
With nothing but soldiers,
Ladies, I and my friend
Trust we will not offend,
Which we'd never intend,
By suggesting we spend —

91

THE CELESTES
(*Excited*)

Oh, spend —

SOLDIER

—this magnificent Sunday —

THE CELESTES
(*A bit deflated*)

Oh, Sunday —

SOLDIER

—with you and your friend.
(SOLDIER *offers his arm. Both* CELESTES *rush to take it;* CELESTE #1 *gets there first.* CELESTE #2 *tries to get in between the* SOLDIERS, *can't, and rather than join the* COMPANION, *takes the arm of* CELESTE #1. THEY *all start to promenade*)

CELESTE #2
(*To* CELESTE #1)

The one on the right's an awful bore . . .

CELESTE #1

He's been in a war.

SOLDIER
(*To* COMPANION)

We may get a meal and we might get more . . .
(CELESTE #1 *shakes free of* CELESTE #2, *grabs the arm of the* SOLDIER, *freeing him from his* COMPANION)

CELESTE #1 *and* SOLDIER
(*To themselves, as* THEY *exit*)

92

It's certainly fine for Sunday . . .
It's certainly fine for Sunday . . .
> (*Dejected*, CELESTE #2 *grabs the* COMPANION)

CELESTE #2
> (As SHE *exits, carrying* COMPANION)

It's certainly fine for Sunday . . .
> (GEORGE *is alone.* HE *moves downstage as* FIFI *rises.* HE *sits*)

GEORGE
> (*Leafing back through his sketches. Sings*)

Mademoiselles . . .
> (*Flips a page*)

You and me, pal . . .
> (*Flips*)

Second bottle . . .
Ah, she looks for me . . .
> (*Flips*)

Bonnet flapping . . .
> (*Flips*)

Yapping . . .
> (*Flips*)

Ruff! . . .
Chicken . . .
Pastry . . .
> (*Licks lip; looks offstage to where* DOT *has exited*)

Yes, she looks for me — good.
Let her look for me to tell me why she left me —
As I always knew she would.
I had thought she understood.
They have never understood,
And no reason that they should.
But if anybody could . . .

Finishing the hat,
How you have to finish the hat.
How you watch the rest of the world
From a window
While you finish the hat.

Mapping out a sky,
What you feel like, planning a sky,
What you feel when voices that come
Through the window
Go
Until they distance and die,
Until there's nothing but sky.

And how you're always turning back too late
From the grass or the stick
Or the dog or the light,
How the kind of woman willing to wait's
Not the kind that you want to find waiting
To return you to the night,
Dizzy from the height,
Coming from the hat,
Studying the hat,
Entering the world of the hat,
Reaching through the world of the hat
Like a window,
Back to this one from that.

Studying a face,
Stepping back to look at a face
Leaves a little space in the way like a window,
But to see —
It's the only way to see.

And when the woman that you wanted goes,
You can say to yourself, "Well, I give what I give."
But the woman who won't wait for you knows
That, however you live,
There's a part of you always standing by,
Mapping out the sky,
Finishing a hat . . .
Starting on a hat . . .
Finishing a hat . . .

            (*Showing sketch to* FIFI)

Look, I made a hat . . .
Where there never was a hat . . .

    (MR. *and* MRS. *enter stage right.* THEY *are lost. The*
    BOATMAN *crosses near them and* THEY *stop him in his*
    path)

MR.

Excusez, Masseur. We are lost.

BOATMAN

Huh?

MRS.

Let me try, Daddy.
    (*Slowly and wildly gesticulating with her every word*)
We are alien here. Unable to find passage off island.

BOATMAN
    (*Pointing to the water*)
Why don't you just walk into the water until your lungs fill up
and you die.

    (BOATMAN *crosses away from them, laughing*)

I detest these people.

(*Spotting* LOUIS, *who has entered in search of* DOT)
Isn't that the baker?

Why, yes it is!

> (THEY *cross to* LOUIS. GEORGE *brings on the* HORN
> PLAYER *cut-out.* OLD LADY *enters*)

Where is that tree? Nurse? NURSE!

> (*Horn call.* DOT *enters, and suddenly* SHE *and* GEORGE
> *are still, staring at one another.* EVERYONE *onstage
> turns slowly to them.* PEOPLE *begin to sing fragments
> of songs.* DOT *and* GEORGE *move closer to one another,
> circling each other like gun duellers. The others close
> in around them until* DOT *and* GEORGE *stop, opposite
> each other. Silence.* DOT *takes her bustle and de-
> fiantly turns it around, creating a pregnant stance.
> There is an audible gasp from the onlookers. Blackout*)

> (*Music. Lights slowly come up on* GEORGE *in his stu-
> dio, painting.* DOT *enters and joins* GEORGE *behind the
> painting.* HE *continues painting as* SHE *watches.* HE
> *stops for a moment when* HE *sees her, then continues
> working*)

You are almost finished.

If I do not change my mind again. And you?

DOT

Two more months.

GEORGE

You cannot change your mind.

DOT

Nor do I want to.
                              (*Beat*)
Is it going to be exhibited?

GEORGE

I am not sure. Jules is coming over to look at it. Any minute, in fact.

DOT

Oh, I hope you don't mind my coming.

GEORGE

What is it that you want, Dot?

DOT

George. I would like my painting.

GEORGE

Your painting?

DOT

The one of me powdering.

GEORGE

I did not know that it was yours.

DOT

You said once that I could have it.

GEORGE

In my sleep?

DOT

I want something to remember you by.

GEORGE

You don't have enough now?

DOT

I want the painting, too.
> (GEORGE *stops painting*)

GEORGE

I understand you and Louis are getting married.

DOT

Yes.

GEORGE

He must love you very much to take you in that condition.

DOT

He does.

GEORGE

I didn't think you would go through with it. I did not think that
was what you really wanted.

DOT

I don't think I can have what I really want. Louis is what I think
I need.

GEORGE

Yes. Louis will take you to the Follies! Correct?

George, I didn't come here to argue.
> (JULES *and* YVONNE *enter*)

JULES

George?

GEORGE

Back here, Jules.

DOT

I will go.

GEORGE

Don't leave! It will only be a minute —

JULES
> (*Crossing behind canvas to* GEORGE)

There you are. I brought Yvonne along.

YVONNE

May I take a peek?

DOT

I will wait in the other room.

YVONNE
> (*Sees* DOT)

I hope we are not interrupting you.
> (SHE *and* JULES *step back and study the painting.*
> GEORGE *looks at* DOT *as* SHE *exits to the front room*)

JULES

It is so large. How can you get any perspective? And this light . . .
> (GEORGE *pulls a lantern close to the canvas*)

GEORGE

Stand here.

YVONNE

Extraordinary! Excuse me.

> (YVONNE *exits into the other room.* DOT *is sitting at
> her vanity, which is now cleared of her belongings.*
> YVONNE *and* DOT *look at each other for a moment*)

Talk of painting bores me. It is hard to escape it when you are
with an artist.

> (*Beat*)

I do not know how you can walk up all those steps in your condition. I remember when I had Louise. I could never be on my
feet for long periods of time. Certainly could never navigate steps.

DOT

Did someone carry you around?

YVONNE

Why are you so cool to me?

DOT

Maybe I don't like you.

YVONNE

Whatever have I done to make you feel that way?

DOT

"Whatever have I done . . . ?" Maybe it is the way you speak.
What are you really doing here?

YVONNE

You know why we are here. So Jules can look at George's work.

100

DOT

I do not understand why George invites you. He knows you do not like his painting.

YVONNE

That is not entirely true. Jules has great respect for George. And he has encouraged him since they were in school.

DOT

That is not what I hear. Jules is jealous of George now.

YVONNE
(*Beat*)

Well . . . jealousy is a form of flattery, is it not? I have been jealous of you on occasion.
(DOT *looks surprised*)
When I have seen George drawing you in the park. Jules has rarely sketched me.

DOT

You are his wife.

YVONNE
(*Uncomfortable*)

Too flat. Too angular.

DOT

Modeling is hard work. You wouldn't like it anyway.

YVONNE

It is worth it, don't you think?

DOT

Sometimes . . .

101

YVONNE

Has your life changed much now that you are with the baker?

DOT

I suppose. He enjoys caring for me.

YVONNE

You are very lucky. Oh, I suppose Jules cares — but there are times when he just does not know Louise and I are there. George always seems so oblivious to everyone.
(*Lowers her voice*)
Jules says that is what is wrong with his painting. Too obsessive. You have to have a life! Don't you agree?
(DOT *nods*)

JULES

George . . . I do not know what to say. What *is* this?

GEORGE

What is the dominant color? The flower on the hat?

JULES

Is this a school exam, George?

GEORGE

What is that color?

JULES
(*Bored*)

Violet.
(GEORGE *takes him by the hand and moves him closer to the canvas*)

102

GEORGE

See? Red and blue. Your eye made the violet.

JULES

So?

GEORGE

So, your eye is perceiving both red and blue *and* violet. Only eleven colors — no black — divided, not mixed on the palette, mixed by the eye. Can't you see the shimmering?

JULES

George . . .

GEORGE

Science, Jules. Fixed laws for color, like music.

JULES

You are a painter, not a scientist! You cannot even see these faces!

GEORGE

I am not painting faces! I am —

JULES

George! I have touted your work in the past, and now you are embarrassing me! People are talking —

GEORGE

Why should I paint like you or anybody else? I am trying to get through to something new. Something that is my own.

103

JULES

And I am trying to understand.

GEORGE

And I want you to understand. Look at the canvas, Jules. Really look at it.

JULES

George! Let us get to the point. You have invited me here because you want me to try to get this included in the next group show.

GEORGE
(*Beat — embarrassed*)
It will be finished soon. I want it to be seen.
    (YVONNE, *who has been eavesdropping at the studio door, leans into the room*)

YVONNE

Jules, I am sorry to interrupt, but we really must be going. You know we have an engagement.

JULES

Yes.

YVONNE

Thank you, George.

JULES

Yes. Thank you.

GEORGE

Yes. Thank you for coming.

JULES

I will give the matter some thought.

> (THEY *exit.* GEORGE *stands motionless for a moment staring at the canvas, then dives into his work, painting the girls)*

GEORGE

He does not like you. He does not understand or appreciate you. He can only see you as everyone else does. Afraid to take you apart and put you back together again for himself. But we will not let anyone deter us, will we?

> *(Hums)*

Bumbum bum bumbumbum bumbum —

DOT

(Calling to him)

George!

> (GEORGE, *embarrassed, crosses in front of canvas.* HE *begins to speak.* DOT *tries to interrupt him)*

GEORGE	DOT
Excuse me — speaking with Jules about the painting — well, I just picked up my brushes — I do not believe he even looked at the painting, though —	You asked me to stay, George, and then you forget that I am even here. George!

DOT

I have something to tell you.

GEORGE

Yes. Now, about "your" painting —

DOT

I may be going away.

(*Beat*)

To America.

GEORGE

Alone.

DOT

Of course not! With Louis. He has work.

GEORGE

When?

DOT

After the baby arrives.

GEORGE

You will not like it there.

DOT

How do you know?

GEORGE

(*Getting angry*)

I have read about America. Why are you telling me this? First, you ask for a painting that is *not* yours — then you tell me this.

(*Beginning to return to the studio*)

I have work to do.

(*Chord; music continues under*)

DOT

Yes, George, run to your work. Hide behind your painting. I have come to tell you I am leaving because I thought you might

106

care to know — foolish of me, because you care about nothing —

GEORGE

I care about many things —

DOT

Things — not people.

GEORGE

People, too. I cannot divide my feelings up as neatly as you, and I am not hiding behind my canvas — I am living in it.

DOT
(*Sings*)
What you care for is yourself.

GEORGE

I care about this painting. *You* will be in this painting.

DOT

I am something you can use.

GEORGE
(*Sings*)
I had thought you understood.

DOT

It's because I understand that I left,
That I am leaving.

GEORGE

Then there's nothing I can say,
Is there?

107

Yes, George, there is!
You could tell me not to go.
Say it to me,
Tell me not to go.
Tell me that you're hurt,
Tell me you're relieved,
Tell me that you're bored —
Anything, but don't assume I know.
Tell me what you feel!

GEORGE

What I feel?
You know exactly how I feel.
Why do you insist
You must hear the words,
When you know I cannot give you words?
Not the ones you need.

There's nothing to say.
I cannot be what you want.

DOT

What do *you* want, George?

GEORGE

I needed you and you left.

DOT

There was no room for me —

GEORGE
(*Overriding her*)

You will not accept who I am.
I am what I do —

108

Which you knew,
Which you always knew,
Which I thought you were a part of!
              (HE *goes behind the canvas*)

                    D O T

No,
You are complete, George,
You are your own.
We do not belong together.
You are complete, George,
You all alone.
I am unfinished,
I am diminished
With or without you.

We do not belong together,
And we should have belonged together.
What made it so right together
Is what made it all wrong.

No one is you, George,
There we agree,
But others will do, George.
No one is you and
No one can be,
But no one is me, George,
No one is me.
We do not belong together.
And we'll never belong — !

You have a mission,
A mission to see.

Now I have one too, George.
And we should have belonged together.

I have to move on.

> (DOT *leaves.* GEORGE *stops painting and comes from around the canvas.* HE *is left standing alone onstage. The lights fade*)

> (*The set changes back to the park scene around him. When the change is complete,* HE *moves downstage right with the* OLD LADY, *and begins to draw her.* THEY *are alone, except for the cut-out of the* COMPANION, *which stands towards the rear of the stage. There is a change of tone in both* GEORGE *and the* OLD LADY. SHE *has assumed a kind of loving attitude, soft and dreamlike.* GEORGE *is rather sullen in her presence*)

OLD LADY
(*Staring across the water*)

I remember when you were a little boy. You would rise up early on a Sunday morning and go for a swim . . .

GEORGE

I do not know how to swim.

OLD LADY

The boys would come by the house to get you . . .

GEORGE

I have always been petrified of the water.

OLD LADY

And your father would walk you all to the banks of the Seine . . .

GEORGE

Father was never faithful to us.

OLD LADY

And he would give you boys careful instruction, telling you just how far to swim out . . .

GEORGE

And he certainly never instructed.

OLD LADY

And now, look across there — in the distance — all those beautiful trees cut down for a foolish tower.
(*Music under*)

GEORGE

I do not think there were ever trees there.

OLD LADY

How I loved the view from here . . .
(*Sings*)
  Changing . . .

GEORGE

I am quite certain that was an open field . . .

OLD LADY

  It keeps changing.

GEORGE

I used to play there as a child.

OLD LADY

  I see towers
  Where there were trees.

Going,
All the stillness,
The solitude,
Georgie.

Sundays,
Disappearing
All the time,
When things were beautiful . . .

All things are beautiful,
Mother.
All trees, all towers,
Beautiful.
That tower —
Beautiful, Mother,
See?

(Gestures)
A perfect tree.

Pretty isn't beautiful, Mother,
Pretty is what changes.
What the eye arranges
Is what is beautiful.

Fading . . .

I'm changing.
You're changing.

OLD LADY

It keeps fading . . .

GEORGE

I'll draw us now before we fade, Mother.

OLD LADY

It keeps melting
Before our eyes.

GEORGE

You watch
While I revise the world.

OLD LADY

Changing,
As we sit here —
Quick, draw it all,
Georgie!

OLD LADY *and* GEORGE

Sundays —

OLD LADY

Disappearing,
As we look —

GEORGE

Look! . . . Look! . . .

OLD LADY
(*Not listening, fondly*)

You make it beautiful.

113

(*Music continues*)
Oh, Georgie, how I long for the old view.
>(*Music out. The* SOLDIER *and* CELESTE #2 *enter arm-in-arm and promenade*)

SOLDIER
(*Noticing his* COMPANION)
I am glad to be free of him.

CELESTE #2
Friends can be confining.

SOLDIER
He never understood my moods.

CELESTE #2
She only thought of herself.
>(MR. *and* MRS. *enter.* HE *is carrying a big steamer trunk.*
>SHE *is carrying a number of famous paintings, framed,*
>*under her arm.* THEY *are followed by* DOT, *who is car-*
>*rying her* BABY *bundled in white, and* LOUIS)

SOLDIER
It felt as if I had this
burden at my side.

CELESTE #2
She never really cared
about me.

SOLDIER
We had very different tastes.

MR.
This damned island again!
I do not understand why we
are not goin' straight to
our boat.

MRS.
They wanted to come here
first.

CELESTE #2
She had no taste.

MR.
That much I figured out —
but why? Didn't you ask
them?

SOLDIER
She did seem rather pushy.

MRS.
I don't know.

CELESTE #2
Very! And he was so odd.

SOLDIER
(*Angry*)
HE IS NOT ODD!

(MR. *and* MRS. *are stopped*
by the SOLDIER'*s line,*
"*He is not odd.*")

CELESTE #2
No. No, I didn't really mean odd . . .
(THEY *exit.* LOUISE *runs onstage.* BOATMAN *rushes after*
her)

BOATMAN
(*Mutters as* HE *chases after* LOUISE)
. . . you better not let me get my hands on you.
(HE *chases her offstage*)

MR.
Are we ever going to get home?!
(MR. *and* MRS. *exit.* DOT *crosses downstage to* GEORGE)

GEORGE
(*Not looking up*)
You are blocking my light.

115

DOT

Marie and I came to watch.

GEORGE
(*Turning towards* DOT)

Marie . . .

(*Back to his sketch pad*)

You know I do not like anyone staring over my shoulder.

DOT

Yes, I know.

(SHE *moves to another position*)

George, we are about to leave for America. I have come to ask for the painting of me powdering again. I would like to take it with me.

GEORGE
(HE *stops for a moment*)

Oh? I have repainted it.

(HE *draws*)

DOT

What.

GEORGE

Another model.

DOT

You knew I wanted it.

GEORGE

Perhaps if you had remained still —

116

DOT

Perhaps if you would look up from your pad! What is wrong with you, George? Can you not even look at your own child?

GEORGE

She is not my child. Louis is her father.

DOT

Louis is not her father.

GEORGE

Louis is her father now. Louis will be a loving and attentive father. I cannot because I cannot look up from my pad.
> (SHE *stands speechless for a moment, then begins to walk away*; GEORGE *turns to her*)

Dot.
> (SHE *stops*)

I *am* sorry.
> (DOT *and* LOUIS *exit.* GEORGE *drawing* OLD LADY)

OLD LADY

I worry about you, George.

GEORGE

Could you turn slightly toward me, please.
> (SHE *does so*)

OLD LADY

No future in dreaming.

GEORGE

Drop the head a little, please.

(SHE *does so.* CELESTE #1 *enters and goes to the* COMPANION)

OLD LADY

I worry about you and that woman, too.

GEORGE

I have another woman in my life now.

OLD LADY

They are all the same woman.

GEORGE
(*Chuckles*)

Variations on a theme.

OLD LADY

Ah, you always drifted as a child.

GEORGE
(*Muttering*)

Shadows are too heavy.

OLD LADY

You were always in some other place — seeing something no one else could see.

GEORGE

Softer light.

(*Lights dim slowly*)

OLD LADY

We tried to get through to you, George. Really we did.

118

(GEORGE *stops drawing.* HE *looks at her. Looks at the page*)

GEORGE
(*Laments*)

Connect, George.

(*Trails off*)

Connect . . .

(FRIEDA *and* JULES *enter.* THEY *seem to be hiding*)

FRIEDA

Are you certain you wish to do this?

JULES
(*Uncertain*)

Of course. We just have to find a quiet spot. I've wanted to do it outside for a long time.

FRIEDA

Franz would kill you —

JULES
(*Panics*)

Is he in the park?

FRIEDA

I am not certain.

JULES

Oh. Well. Perhaps some other day would be better.

FRIEDA

Some other day? Always some other day. Perhaps you do not really wish to —

JULES
(*Subservient*)

I do. I do! I love tall grass.

FRIEDA

Ja. Tall grass. You wouldn't toy with my affections, would you?

JULES

No. No. Of course not.

FRIEDA

I see a quiet spot over there.

JULES
(*Pointing where* SHE *did, nervous*)

Over there. There are people in that grove —
　　　(FRIEDA *places his hand on her breast.* THEY *are inter-*
　　　rupted by the entrance of CELESTE #2 *and the* SOL-
　　　DIER. FRIEDA, *then* JULES, *exits; as* HE *leaves*)

Bon jour.

SOLDIER

Do you suppose there is a violation being perpetrated by that man?

CELESTE #2

What?

SOLDIER

There is something in the air today . . .

CELESTE #1
(*To the* COMPANION)

Being alone is nothing new for me.

120

SOLDIER
(*Noticing* CELESTE #1)

Look who is watching us.

CELESTE #1

Sundays are such a bore. I'd almost rather be in the shop. Do you like your work? I hate mine!

CELESTE #2

I do not care if she never speaks to me again.

SOLDIER

She won't.
(*Chord.* FRANZ *and the* NURSE *enter as if to rendez-vous*)

YVONNE
(*Entering*)

FRANZ!
(NURSE *exits.* YVONNE *goes to* FRANZ)

Franz, have you seen Louise?

FRANZ
(*Angry*)

Nein, Madame.

YVONNE

I thought Frieda was going to care for her today.

FRANZ

But it's Sunday.

YVONNE

What of it?

121

FRANZ

Our day off!

YVONNE

Oh. But I have just lost my little girl!
(FRANZ *shrugs his shoulders and begins looking for* LOUISE)

SOLDIER

Let's go say hello to Celeste.

YVONNE
(*Calling*)

Louise?

CELESTE #2
(*Indignant*)

I do not wish to speak with her!

SOLDIER

Come. It will be fun!
(SOLDIER *takes* CELESTE #2 *toward* CELESTE #1. LOUISE *comes running in breathless.*)

YVONNE

Louise! Where have you been, young lady?!

LOUISE

With Frieda.

YVONNE
(*To* FRANZ)

There, you see.

122

FRANZ

Frieda?

LOUISE

And with Father.

YVONNE

Your father is in the studio.

LOUISE

No, he's not. He's with Frieda. I saw them.

FRANZ

Where?

LOUISE

Over there. Tonguing.
(FRANZ *exits. Music under, agitated*)

OLD LADY

Manners. Grace. Respect.

YVONNE
(*Beginning to spank* LOUISE)
How dare you, young lady!

LOUISE   (SOLDIER *and* CELESTE #2
It's true. It's true!   *reach* CELESTE #1)

                                CELESTE #1
(JULES *enters, somewhat*   What do you want?
sheepishly)

                                SOLDIER
                                We've come for a visit.

123

YVONNE
Where the hell have you
been? What are you doing
here?

CELESTE #1
I don't want to say hello to
her. Cheap Christmas
wrapping.

JULES
Darling, I came out here
looking for Louise.

CELESTE #2
Cheap! Look who is talking.
You have the worst reputation
of anyone in Paris.

LOUISE
(*Crying*)
You came to tongue.

CELESTE #1
At least I have a reputation.
You could not draw a fly
to flypaper!

(BOATMAN *enters and begins chasing* LOUISE *around the stage.* MR. *and* MRS. *enter and are caught up in the frenzy. All hell breaks loose,* EVERYONE *speaking at once, the stage erupting into total chaos*)

YVONNE
How dare you, Jules!
(SHE *goes to him and begins
striking him*)

SOLDIER
Ladies, you mustn't fight.

CELESTE #2
I seem to be doing just
fine.

JULES
Nothing, I swear.

CELESTE #1
Hah. With a diseased
soldier!

YVONNE
Nothing. Look.
(FRANZ *drags in* FRIEDA)

SOLDIER
Wait just a minute.

Have you been with my
husband?

CELESTE #1
Disgusting sores everywhere.

FRIEDA
Madame, he gave me no
choice.

CELESTE #2
Don't say that about him.

FRANZ
What do you mean he gave
you no choice?

SOLDIER
Yes, don't say that —

JULES
(Letting go of LOUISE, *who
drifts off to the side)*
That is not so. Your wife
lured me.

CELESTE #1
I'll say whatever I like.
You are both ungrateful,
cheap, ugly, diseased,
disgusting garbage . . .

FRIEDA
Lured you! You all but forced
me —

SOLDIER
Listen here, lady, if in
fact there is anything
ladylike about you. You
should be glad to take what
you can get, any way you
can get it and I —

JULES
You are both fired!

FRANZ
FIRED! You think we would
continue to work in your
house?

CELESTE #2
You think you know every-
thing. You are not so
special, and far from as
pretty as you think, and
everyone that comes into
the shop knows exactly what
you are and what —

YVONNE
Jules, you cannot change the
subject. What were you
doing?

(EVERYONE *has slowly fought their way to the middle of the stage, creating one big fight.* GEORGE *and the* OLD LADY *have been watching the chaos.* GEORGE *begins to cross stage to exit. Arpeggiated chord, as at the beginning of the play.* EVERYBODY *suddenly freezes*)

Remember, George.
> (*Another chord.* GEORGE *turns to the group*)

Order.
> (*Another chord.* EVERYONE *turns simultaneously to* GEORGE. *As chords continue under,* HE *nods to them, and* THEY *each take up a position on stage*)

Design.
> (*Chord.* GEORGE *nods to* FRIEDA *and* FRANZ, *and* THEY *cross downstage right onto the apron. Chord.* GEORGE *nods to* MR. *and* MRS., *and* THEY *cross upstage*)

Tension.
> (*Chord.* GEORGE *nods to* CELESTE #1 *and* CELESTE #2, *and* THEY *cross downstage. Another chord.* JULES *and* YVONNE *cross upstage*)

Balance.
> (*Chord.* OLD LADY *crosses right as* DOT *and* LOUIS *cross center.* GEORGE *signals* LOUIS *away from* DOT. *Another chord.* SOLDIER *crosses upstage left;* LOUISE, *upstage right. Chord.* GEORGE *gestures to the* BOATMAN, *who crosses downstage right*)

Harmony.
> (*The music becomes calm, stately, triumphant.* GEORGE *turns front. The promenade begins. Throughout the*

song, GEORGE *is moving about, setting trees, cut-outs,*
and figures — making a perfect picture)

ALL

Sunday,
By the blue
Purple yellow red water
On the green
Purple yellow red grass,
Let us pass
Through our perfect park,
Pausing on a Sunday
By the cool
Blue triangular water
On the soft
Green elliptical grass
As we pass
Through arrangements of shadows
Towards the verticals of trees
Forever . . .

(The horn sounds)

By the blue
Purple yellow red water
On the green
Orange violet mass
Of the grass
In our perfect park,

GEORGE
(To DOT*)*

Made of flecks of light
And dark,
And parasols:

127

Bumbum bum bumbumbum
Bumbum bum . . .

ALL
People strolling through the trees
Of a small suburban park
On an island in the river
On an ordinary Sunday . . .
(The horn sounds. Chimes. THEY *all reach their positions)*
Sunday . . .
(The horn again. EVERYONE *assumes the final pose of the painting.* GEORGE *comes out to the apron)*
Sunday . . .
(At the last moment, GEORGE *rushes back and removes* LOUISE's *eyeglasses.* HE *dashes back on to the apron and freezes the picture. Final chord. The completed canvas flies in. Very slow fade, as the image of the characters fades behind the painting with* GEORGE *in front. Blackout)*

George and Dot

DOT: *A trickle of sweat.*
The back of the head.
He always does this.
Now the foot is dead.
Sunday in the park with George.

GEORGE: *Look out at the water. Not at me.*

George corrects Dot's pose, as Nurse reads to Old Lady.

Georges Seurat's painting "Bathing at Asnières" (1883–84)

The tableau-vivant of it as presented on stage

Yvonne and Jules

Opposite page: *In his studio George works on the canvas of the painting while Dot at her vanity sings of what it would be like to be a Folly girl.* Below: *Seurat's "Woman Powdering Herself" (1889–90).*

Frieda and Franz; the Celestes, Nurse, Soldier with Companion, Jules

Mr. and Mrs., an American southern couple

*Soldier with Companion
and the Celestes*

Louis and Dot

George sketching the Boatman; in background, Yvonne and Jules with their daughter Louise, Nurse and Old Lady, Louis and Dot, the Celestes. Below: Old Lady and George.

Dot comes to George's studio and, in the song "We Do Not Belong Together," tries to make him understand why she had to leave him.

Left is Georges Seurat's painting "A Sunday Afternoon on the Island of La Grande Jatte." Below it is the tableau suggested by the painting, posed onstage at the end of Act I. The tableau characters, left to right, are:

1 Boatman, reclining
2 Franz, in top hat
3 Frieda, sitting
4 Celeste #1, fishing
5 Nurse, back to camera
6 Old Lady, seated, holding parasol
7 Soldier
8 Louise
9 Yvonne, holding parasol
10 Woman, seated, wearing dark hat
11 Man, seated, wearing black bowler
12 Celeste #2, seated, hatless
13 Louis, holding baby
14 Mr., wearing light suit
15 Jules, wearing black topper
16 Dot, holding parasol

The two dogs and the monkey are two-dimensional cut-out silhouettes, as are the figures of a man (partly hidden behind Celeste #1), a woman with parasol standing in background left and one seated in foreground right center, a child in front of Mr., and a woman seated at extreme right.

Bran Ferren

Marie gives George some of her mother's advice :

    . . . "Honey,
Mustn't be blue.
It's not so much do what you like
As it is that you like what you do."

Opposite page, top: *The presentation of Chromolume #7 with George at the console and Marie.* Bottom: *In the song "Putting It Together," George sings about the sacrifices involved in "the art of making art." (Behind George is a cut-out of him. At right are Elaine and Marie.)*

DOT: *Anything you do,*
Let it come from you.
Then it will be new.
Give us more to see . . .

ACT II

Lights fade up slowly, and we see EVERYONE *in the tableau. There is a very long pause before we begin. The audience should feel the tension. Finally, music begins.*

DOT
(*Sings*)

It's hot up here.

YVONNE

It's hot and it's monotonous.

LOUISE

I want my glasses.

FRANZ

This is not my good profile.

NURSE

Nobody can even *see* my profile.

CELESTE #1

I hate this dress.

CELESTE #2

The soldiers have forgotten us.

FRIEDA

The boatman *schwitzes*.

JULES

I am completely out of proportion.

SOLDIER

These helmets weigh a lot on us.

OLD LADY

This tree is blocking my view.

LOUISE

I can't see anything.

BOATMAN

Why are they complaining?
It could have been raining.

DOT

I hate these people.

ALL

It's hot up here
A lot up here.
It's hot up here
Forever.

A lot of fun
It's not up here.

132

It's hot up here,
No matter what.

There's not a breath
Of air up here,
And they're up here
Forever.

It's not my fault
I got up here.
I'll rot up here,
I am so hot up here.

YVONNE
(To LOUISE)

Darling, don't clutch mother's hand quite so tightly. Thank you.

CELESTE #1

It's hot up here.

FRIEDA

At least you have a parasol.

SOLDIER, NURSE, YVONNE, *and* LOUISE

Well, look who's talking,
Sitting in the shade.

JULES
(To DOT)

I trust my cigar is not bothering you — unfortunately, it never
goes out.

(SHE *pays him no attention*)

You have excellent concentration.

SOLDIER
(*To* COMPANION)
It's good to be together again.

CELESTE #2
(*To* CELESTE #1)
See, I told you they were odd.

CELESTE #1
Don't slouch.

LOUISE
He took my glasses!

YVONNE
You've been eating something sticky.

NURSE
I put on rouge today, too . . .

FRIEDA
(*To* BOATMAN)
Don't you ever take a bath?

OLD LADY
Nurse! Hand me my fan.

NURSE
I can't.

FRANZ
At least the brat is with her mother.

134

LOUISE

I heard that!

JULES
(*To* DOT)

Do you like tall grass?

FRIEDA

Hah!

YVONNE

Jules!

BOATMAN

Bunch of animals . . .

DOT

I hate these people.

ALL

It's hot up here
And strange up here,
No change up here
Forever.

How still it is,
How odd it is,
And God, it is
So hot!

SOLDIER

I like the one in the light hat.

135

Hello, George.
I do not wish to be remembered
Like this, George,
With them, George.
My hem, George:
Three inches off the ground
And then this monkey
And these people, George —

They'll argue till they fade
And whisper things and grunt.
But thank you for the shade,
And putting me in front.
Yes, thank you, George, for that . . .

And for the hat . . .

CELESTE #1

It's hot up here.

YVONNE

It's hot and it's monotonous.

LOUISE

I want my glasses!

FRANZ

This is not my good profile.

CELESTE #1

I hate this dress.

136

(Overlapping)

CELESTE #2
The soldiers have forgotten us.

CELESTE #1
Don't slouch!

BOATMAN
Animals . . .

JULES
Are you sure you don't like tall grass?

NURSE
I put on rouge today, too . . .

FRIEDA
Don't you ever take a bath?

SOLDIER
It's good to be together again.

OLD LADY
Nurse, hand me my fan.

DOT
It's hot up here.

YVONNE
It's hot and it's monotonous.

137

LOUISE

He took my glasses, I want my glasses!

FRANZ

This is not my good profile.

ALL

And furthermore,
Finding you're
Fading
Is very degrading
And God, I am so hot!

Well, there are worse things than sweating
By a river on a Sunday.
There are worse things than sweating by a river

BOATMAN

When you're sweating in a picture
That was painted by a genius

FRANZ

And you know that you're immortal

FRIEDA

And you'll always be remembered

NURSE

Even if they never see you

OLD LADY

And you're listening to drivel

SOLDIER
And you're part of your companion

LOUISE
And your glasses have been stolen

YVONNE
And you're bored beyond endurance

LOUIS
And the baby has no diapers

CELESTE #1
(*To* CELESTE #2)
And you're slouching

CELESTE #2
I am not!

JULES
And you are out of all proportion

DOT
And I hate these people!

ALL
You never get
A breeze up here,
And she's (he's) up here
Forever.

You cannot run
Amok up here,

139

You're stuck up here
In this gavotte.

Perspectives don't
Make sense up here.
It's tense up here
Forever.

The outward show
Of bliss up here
Is disappear-
Ing dot by dot.

        (Long pause. Music continues endlessly)
And it's hot!

    (THEY *shake themselves loose from the pose for a brief
moment but at the last beat of the music resume their
positions.* During the following, the* CHARACTERS *break
from their poses when* THEY *speak. Accompanying their
exits, pieces of scenery disappear; by the time the*
BOATMAN *exits at the end of the sequence, the set is
returned to its original white configuration)*

CELESTE #2

Thirty-one . . .

CELESTE #1

It is hard to believe.

CELESTE #2

Yes.

CELESTE #1

It seems like only yesterday we were posing for him.

  * See page 203.

140

CELESTE #2

We never posed for him!

CELESTE #1

Certainly we did! We are in a painting, aren't we?

CELESTE #2

It's not as if he asked us to sit!

CELESTE #1

If you had sat up —

SOLDIER

Will you two just keep QUIET!
(HE *steps downstage. The* CELESTES *exit*)
I hardly knew the man. I would spend my Sundays here, and I would see him sketching, so I was surprised when he stopped showing up. Of course, I did not notice right away. But one day, I realized, something was different — like a flash of light, right through me, the way that man would stare at you when he sketched — I knew, he was no longer.
(SOLDIER *exits.* LOUISE *breaks away from her* MOTHER *and dashes downstage*)

LOUISE

I am going to be a painter when I grow up!

BOATMAN

If you live.
(LOUISE *runs off*)

FRIEDA

Honestly!

141

BOATMAN

Keep your mouth shut!

FRIEDA

It is my mouth and I shall do as I please!

FRANZ

Quiet! George was a gentleman.

FRIEDA

Soft spoken.

FRANZ

And he was a far superior artist to Monsieur.

FRIEDA

George had beautiful eyes.

FRANZ

Ja, he — beautiful eyes?

FRIEDA

Ja . . . well . . . eyes that captured beauty.

FRANZ
(*Suspicious*)

Ja . . . he chose his subjects well.
(THEY *exit*)

DOT

I was in Charleston when I heard. At first, I was surprised by
the news. Almost relieved, in fact. Perhaps I knew this is how
it would end — perhaps we both knew.
(SHE *exits*)

A parent wants to die first. But George was always off and running, and I was never able to keep up with him.

No one knew he was ill until the very last days. I offered to care for him, but he would let no one near. Not even her.

(OLD LADY *and* NURSE *exit*)

(*Too sincere*)

George had great promise as a painter. It really is a shame his career was ended so abruptly. He had an unusual flair for color and light, and his work was not as mechanical as some have suggested. I liked George. He was dedicated to his work — seldom did anything but work — and I am proud to have counted him among my friends.

George stopped me once in the park — it was the only time I had ever spoken to him outside the company of Jules. He stared at my jacket for an instant, then muttered something about beautiful colors and just walked on. I rather fancied George.

(JULES *looks at her*)

Well, most of the women did!

(JULES *and* YVONNE *exit*)

They all wanted him and hated him at the same time. They wanted to be painted — splashed on some fancy salon wall. But they hated him, too. Hated him because he only spoke when he absolutely had to. Most of all, they hated him because they knew he would always be around.

(BOATMAN *exits. The stage is bare.*)

(Lights change. Electronic music. It is 1984. We are in the auditorium of the museum where the painting now hangs. Enter GEORGE. *HE wheels in his grandmother,* MARIE *[played by* DOT*], who is ninety-eight and confined to a wheelchair.* DENNIS, GEORGE's *technical assistant, rolls on a control console and places it stage right. An immense white machine rolls on and comes to rest center stage. Our contemporary* GEORGE *is an inventor-sculptor, and this is his latest invention, Chromolume #7. The machine is post-modern in design and is dominated by a four-foot-in-diameter sphere at the top. It glows a range of cool colored light.* MARIE *sits on one side of the machine, and* GEORGE *stands at the console on the other. Behind them is a full-stage projection screen)*

GEORGE

Ladies and gentlemen, in 1983 I was commissioned by this museum to create an art piece commemorating Georges Seurat's painting "A Sunday Afternoon on the Island of La Grande Jatte." My latest Chromolume stands before you now, the seventh in a continuing series. Because I have a special association with this painting, the museum director, Robert Greenberg, suggested I assemble a short presentation to precede the activation of my latest invention. I have brought my grandmother along to give me a hand.

(Introducing her)

My grandmother, Marie.

(What follows is a coordinated performance of music, text [read from index cards by GEORGE *and* MARIE*], film projections of the images referred to, and light emissions from the machine. The first section is accompanied by film projections)*

144

MARIE

I was born in Paris, France, ninety-eight years ago. My grandson, George.

GEORGE

I was born in Lodi, New Jersey, thirty-two years ago.

MARIE

My mother was married to Louis, a baker. They left France when I was an infant to travel to Charleston, South Carolina.

GEORGE

Georges Seurat.

MARIE

Born: December 2, 1859.

GEORGE

It was through his mother that the future artist was introduced to the lower-class Parisian parks. Seurat received a classical training at the Beaux Arts.

MARIE

Like his father, he was not an easy man to know.

GEORGE

He lived in an age when science was gaining influence over Romantic principles.

MARIE

He worked very hard.

GEORGE

His first painting, at the age of twenty-four, "Bathing at Asnières," was rejected by the Salon, but was shown by the Group of Independent Artists.

MARIE

They hung it over the refreshment stand.
(*Ad-libbing*)
Wasn't that awful?

GEORGE

On Ascension Day 1884, he began work on his second painting, "A Sunday Afternoon on the Island of La Grande Jatte." He was to work two years on this painting.

MARIE

He always knew where he was going before he picked up a paint brush.

GEORGE

He denied conventional perspective and conventional space.

MARIE

He was unconventional in his lifestyle as well.
(*Ad-libbing again*)
So was I! You know I was a Florodora Girl for a short time — when I left Charleston and before I was married to my first husband —

GEORGE
(*Interrupting her*)
Marie. Marie!
(SHE *looks over to him*)
The film is running.

146

MARIE

Excuse me.

(SHE *reads*)

They hung it over the refreshment stand.

GEORGE

Marie!

(HE *reads*)

Having studied scientific findings on color, he developed a new style of painting. He found by painting tiny particles, color next to color, that at a certain distance the eye would fuse the specks optically, giving them greater intensity than any mixed pigments.

MARIE

He wanted to paint with colored lights.

GEORGE

Beams of colored light, he hoped.

MARIE

It was shown at the Eighth and last Impressionist Exhibition.

GEORGE

Monet, Renoir, and Sisley withdrew their submissions because of his painting.

MARIE

They placed it in a small room off to the side of the main hall, too dark for the painting to truly be seen.

GEORGE

The painting was ridiculed by most. But there were also a handful of believers in his work.

He went on to paint six more major paintings before his sudden death at the age of thirty-one. He never sold a painting in his lifetime.

GEORGE

On this occasion, I present my latest Chromolume —

MARIE

— Number Seven —

GEORGE

— which pays homage to "La Grande Jatte" and to my grandmother, Marie. The score for this presentation has been composed by Naomi Eisen.
(NAOMI *enters, bows, and exits*)

MARIE
(SHE *reads a stage direction by mistake*)
George begins to activate the Chromolume machine as . . .

GEORGE

Don't read that part, Grandmother.

MARIE

Oh . . . don't read this . . .
(*Music begins to increase in volume and intensity. Strobe lights begin emitting from the machine along with side shafts of brilliant light. Colors begin to fill the stage and audience, creating a pointillist look. Just as the sphere begins to illuminate, producing various images from the painting, there is a sudden explosion of sparks and smoke. The lighting system flickers on*

*and off until everything dies, including music. There
is a moment of silence in the darkness)*

GEORGE
(*Under his breath*)

Shit.

(*Calling out*)

Robert Greenberg?

GREENBERG
(*From the back of the house*)

Just a minute, George!
(*Some light returns to the smoke-filled stage*)

DENNIS
(*Offstage*)

It's the regulator, George.
(*Lights come up on* GEORGE, *who is looking inside the
machine.* HE *steps downstage toward the audience*)

GEORGE

My apologies, ladies and gentlemen. For precise synchroniza-
tion of all the visual elements, I've installed a new state-of-the-
art Japanese microcomputer which controls the voltage regulator. I think that the surge from the musical equipment has created an electrical short.

(*Beat*)

Unfortunately, no electricity, no art. Give us a moment and we'll
be able to bypass the regulator and be back in business.
(*After "no electricity, no art,"* GREENBERG *has entered
and stands to the side of the apron.* DENNIS *enters and
joins* GEORGE *at the Chromolume*)

149

GREENBERG

I am very sorry, ladies and gentlemen. We seem to be having a little electrical difficulty.

(NAOMI *has entered and rushed to the machine*)

NAOMI

There's no juice!

GREENBERG

You must realize this is the first time we have had a collaboration like this at the museum and it has offered some extraordinary challenges to us here.

(NAOMI *and* DENNIS *exit arguing*)

Now, I hope to see all of you at the reception and dinner which will follow the presentation. It's right down the hall in the main gallery, where the painting hangs. And we have a very special treat for you. As I am sure you have noticed, in order to raise additional funds we have chosen to sell the air rights to the museum — and some of the twenty-seven flights of condominiums that stand above us now will be open for your inspection after dinner. You may even wish to become one of our permanent neighbors!

GEORGE

We're ready, Bob.

GREENBERG

Well . . . proceed. Proceed!

(HE *exits*)

GEORGE
(*Into his headset*)

Dennis! Lights.

150

(Lights dim and the presentation continues. Music gathers momentum. The Chromolume begins before the speaking resumes, with images from the painting projected on its sphere, illustrating the lecture)

MARIE

When I was young, Mother loved telling me tales of her life in France, and of her work as an artist's model.

GEORGE

Her mother showed her this great painting and pointed to this woman and said that it was she.

MARIE

And she pointed to a couple in the back — they were holding an infant child — and she said that was me!

GEORGE

Shortly before my great-grandmother's death, she spoke of her association with the artist of this painting. She told Marie that Seurat was her real father.

MARIE

I was shocked!

GEORGE

My parents never believed this story. After all, there was no proof. I do not —

MARIE

(Produces a red book, unbeknownst to GEORGE)
My mother gave me this small red book.

GEORGE

Marie!

MARIE

Oh, George, I wanted to bring the book and show it.
(*To audience*)
In the back are notes about his great-grandfather, the artist.

GEORGE

Actually, this book is really just a grammar book in the hand-writing of a child, and though there *are* notes in the back which mention a Georges — they could be referring to anyone.

MARIE

But they do not.

GEORGE

I do not know that there is any validity to this story.

MARIE

Of course there is validity!
(*To the audience*)
He has to have everything spelled out for him!

GEORGE

The facts are sketchy. The tales are many. I would like to invite you into *my* "Sunday: Island of Light." It will be on exhibition here in the upstairs gallery for three weeks.
(*Music crescendos, as laser beams burst over the audience. When they complete their course, the sphere begins to turn, sending out a blinding burst of light. The painting flies in*)

152

(We are now in the gallery where the painting hangs and in front of which the reception is beginning. HAR-RIET *and* BILLY *enter, closely followed by* REDMOND, GREENBERG, ALEX, BETTY, *and* NAOMI. *Cocktail music under)*

BILLY

Well, I can't say that *I* understand what that light machine has to do with this painting.

HARRIET

Darling, it's a theme and variation.

BILLY

Oh. Theme and variation.

GREENBERG
(To REDMOND*)*

Times change so quickly.

REDMOND

Lord knows.

GREENBERG

That's the challenge of our work. You never know what movement is going to hit next. Which artist to embrace.
(Rhumba music)

NAOMI

I thought it went very well, except for that electrical screw-up. What did you guys think?

153

ALEX	BETTY
Terrible.	Terrific.

(Short embarrassed pause)

HARRIET
(Sings)
I mean, I don't understand completely —

BILLY
I'm not surprised.

HARRIET
But he combines all these different trends.

BILLY
I'm not surprised.

HARRIET
You can't divide art today
Into categories neatly —

BILLY
Oh.

HARRIET
What matters is the means, not the ends.

BILLY
I'm not surprised.

HARRIET *and* BILLY
That is the state of the art, my dear,
That is the state of the art.

154

GREENBERG

It's not enough knowing good from rotten —

REDMOND

You're telling me —

GREENBERG

When something new pops up every day.

REDMOND

You're telling me —

GREENBERG

It's only new, though, for now —

REDMOND

Nouveau.

GREENBERG

But yesterday's forgotten.

REDMOND
(*Nods*)

And tomorrow is already passé.

GREENBERG

There's no surprise.

REDMOND *and* GREENBERG

That is the state of the art, my friend,
That is the state of the art.

BETTY

He's an original.

ALEX

Was.

NAOMI

I like the images.

ALEX

Some.

BETTY

Come on.
You had your moment,
Now it's George's turn —

ALEX

It's George's turn?
I wasn't talking turns,
I'm talking art.

BETTY
(*To* NAOMI)
Don't you think he's original?

NAOMI

Well, yes . . .

BETTY
(*To* ALEX)
You're talking crap.

ALEX
(*Overlapping with* NAOMI)
But is it really new?

156

NAOMI

Well, no . . .

ALEX
(*To* BETTY)

His own collaborator — !

BETTY
(*Overlapping with* NAOMI)

It's more than novelty.

NAOMI

Well, yes . . .

BETTY
(*To* ALEX)

It's just impersonal, but —

ALEX

It's all promotion, but then —

ALEX *and* BETTY
(*To* NAOMI)

That is the state of the art,
Isn't it?

NAOMI

Well . . .

BILLY
(*To* HARRIET)

Art isn't easy —

157

HARRIET
(*Nodding*)
Even when you've amassed it —

BETTY
Fighting for prizes —

GREENBERG
No one can be an oracle.

REDMOND
(*Nodding*)
Art isn't easy.

ALEX
Suddenly —
(*Snaps fingers*)
You're past it.

NAOMI
All compromises —

HARRIET
(*To* BILLY)
And then when it's allegorical —!

REDMOND *and* GREENBERG
Art isn't easy —

ALL
Any way you look at it.
(*Chord, fanfare.* GEORGE *makes a grand entrance with* MARIE *and* ELAINE. *Applause from* GUESTS. GEORGE *and*

158

(MARIE *move towards the painting. Lights come down on* GEORGE, *who sings*)

GEORGE
All right, George.
As long as it's your night, George . . .
You know what's in the room, George:
Another Chromolume, George.
It's time to get to work . . .
(*Music continues under*)

MARIE
George, look. All these lovely people in front of our painting.

GREENBERG
(*Coming up to* GEORGE)
George, I want you to meet one of our board members.
(HE *steers* GEORGE *over to* BILLY *and* HARRIET)
This is Harriet Pawling.

HARRIET
What a pleasure. And this is my friend, Billy Webster.

BILLY
How do you do.

GREENBERG
Well, I'll just leave you three to chat.
(HE *exits*)

BILLY
Harriet was so impressed by your presentation.

159

HARRIET

This is the third piece of yours I've seen. They are getting so large!

BILLY

What heading does your work fall under?

GEORGE

Most people think of it as sculpture.

BILLY

Sculpture . . .

GEORGE

Actually, I think of myself as an inventor as well as a sculptor.

BILLY

It's so unconventional for sculpture.
(*Lights down on* GEORGE)

GEORGE

Say "cheese," George,
And put them at their ease, George.
You're up on the trapeze, George.
Machines don't grow on trees, George.
Start putting it together . . .
(*Lights up*)

HARRIET

I bet your great-grandfather would be very proud!
(THEY *are joined by* MARIE *and* ELAINE, *who have been nearby and overheard the conversation*)

160

MARIE

Yes. He would have loved this evening.

BILLY

How do you know?

MARIE

I just know. I'm like that.

HARRIET

Hi. I'm Harriet Pawling.

BILLY

Billy Webster.

MARIE

How do you do. This is Elaine — George's former wife.

ELAINE
(*Embarrassed*)

Hello.

MARIE

Elaine is such a darling, I will always think of her as my grand-daughter. I am so happy that these children have remained close. Isn't that nice?

BILLY

Yes. Harriet has just gone through a rather messy divorce —

HARRIET

Bill!

161

(*Awkward pause*)
What a fascinating family you have!

MARIE

Many people say that. George and I are going back to France
next month to visit the island where the painting was made, and
George is going to bring the Lomochrome.
(*Music*)

GEORGE

Chromolume. I've been invited by the government to do a presentation of the machine on the island.

MARIE

George has never been to France.

GEORGE
(*Front*)

Art isn't easy —
    (HE *raises a cut-out of himself in front of* BILLY *and*
    HARRIET *and comes downstage*)
Even when you're hot.

BILLY
(*To cut-out*)

Are these inventions of yours one of a kind?

GEORGE

Advancing art is easy —
                    (*To* BILLY, *but front*)
Yes.

Financing it is not.

162

They take a year to make.

GEORGE
(*Front*)

A vision's just a vision
If it's only in your head.

MARIE

The minute he finishes one, he starts raising money for the next.

GEORGE

If no one gets to see it,
It's as good as dead.

MARIE

Work. Work. Work.

GEORGE

It has to come to light!
(*Music continues under.* GEORGE *crosses to center*)
I put the names of my contributors on the side of each machine.

ELAINE

Some very impressive people!

HARRIET

Well, we must speak further. My family has a foundation and we are always looking for new projects.

GEORGE
(*Front*)

Bit by bit,
Putting it together . . .

Family — it's all you really have.

GEORGE

Piece by piece —
Only way to make a work of art.
Every moment makes a contribution,
Every little detail plays a part.
Having just the vision's no solution,
Everything depends on execution:
Putting it together —
That's what counts.

HARRIET

(*To cut-out*)
Actually, the Board of the Foundation is meeting next week . . .

GEORGE

Ounce by ounce
Putting it together . . .

HARRIET

You'll come to lunch.

GEORGE

Small amounts,
Adding up to make a work of art.
First of all, you need a good foundation,
Otherwise it's risky from the start.
Takes a little cocktail conversation,
But without the proper preparation,

Having just the vision's no solution,
Everything depends on execution.

The art of making art
Is putting it together
Bit by bit . . .
   (*The cut-out remains, as* BILLY *and* HARRIET *talk to it;*
   GEORGE *is cornered by* CHARLES REDMOND. *Music
   continues under*)

REDMOND

We have been hearing about you for some time. We haven't
met. Charles Redmond. County Museum of Texas.

GEORGE

Nice to meet you.

REDMOND

Your work is just tremendous.

GEORGE

Thank you.

REDMOND

I don't mean to bring business up during a social occasion, but
I wanted you to know we're in the process of giving out some
very sizable commissions —

GREENBERG

You're not going to steal him away, are you?
   (GEORGE *signals and another cut-out of himself slides*

165

in from the wings. HE *leaves his drink in its hand, then steps forward)*

GEORGE

Link by link,
Making the connections . . .
Drink by drink,
Fixing and perfecting the design.
Adding just a dab of politician
(Always knowing where to draw the line),
Lining up the funds but in addition
Lining up a prominent commission,
Otherwise your perfect composition
Isn't going to get much exhibition.

Art isn't easy.
Every minor detail
Is a major decision.
Have to keep things in scale,
Have to hold to your vision —
                    (*Pauses for a split second*)
Every time I start to feel defensive,
I remember lasers are expensive.
What's a little cocktail conversation
If it's going to get you your foundation,
Leading to a prominent commission
And an exhibition in addition?
        (*The* GUESTS *promenade briefly, working the room*)

ALL
(*Except* MARIE)

Art isn't easy —

166

ALEX *and* BETTY

Trying to make connections —

ALL

Who understands it — ?

HARRIET *and* BILLY

Difficult to evaluate —

ALL

Art isn't easy —

GREENBERG *and* REDMOND

Trying to form collections —

ALL

Always in transit —

NAOMI
(To whoever will listen)
And then when you have to collaborate — !

ALL

Art isn't easy,
Any way you look at it . . .
(Chord. Cocktail piano. GEORGE *is approached by* LEE
RANDOLPH *with* MARIE)

MARIE

George, you have to meet Mr. Randolph!

RANDOLPH

Hello! Lee Randolph. I handle the public relations for the museum.

167

GEORGE

How do you do.

(NAOMI *joins them*)

NAOMI

There you are, George! Hi, Marie.
(*To* RANDOLPH)
Naomi Eisen.

RANDOLPH

Delighted. You kids made quite a stir tonight.

NAOMI

You see, George — that electrical foul-up didn't hurt our reception.

RANDOLPH

There's a lot of opportunity for some nice press here.
(GEORGE *gestures; a third cut-out of himself rises in front of* NAOMI *and* RANDOLPH. GEORGE *steps forward and sings*)

GEORGE

Dot by dot,
Building up the image.
(*Flash.* PHOTOGRAPHER *starts taking pictures of the cut-out*)
Shot by shot,
Keeping at a distance doesn't pay.
Still, if you remember your objective,
Not give all your privacy away —
(*Flash. Beat;* HE *glances at the first cut-out*)
A little bit of hype can be effective,

168

Long as you can keep it in perspective.
After all, without some recognition
No one's going to give you a commission,
Which will cause a crack in the foundation.
You'll have wasted all that conversation.
(*Music stops suddenly as* DENNIS *comes over, disheveled and apologetic.* DENNIS *is something of a nerd*)

DENNIS

I am really sorry, George.
(*Cocktail music*)
I spoke with Naomi in great detail about how much electricity her synthesizer was going to use — I computed the exact voltage —

GEORGE

Dennis! It's okay.

DENNIS

The laser was beautiful, George.

GEORGE

It was, wasn't it? Now go get yourself a drink, Dennis. Mingle.

DENNIS

George. I have one more thing I wanted to talk to you about. I was going to wait — no, I'll wait —

GEORGE

What?

DENNIS

I'm quitting.

169

(*Music stops suddenly*)

GEORGE

Quitting?

DENNIS

I'm going back to NASA. There is just too much pressure in this line of work.

GEORGE

Dennis, don't make any rash decisions. Relax, sleep on it, and we'll talk about it tomorrow.

DENNIS

Okay, George.

GEORGE
(*Front. Music under*)

Art isn't easy . . .
(ALEX *and* BETTY *approach*)

BETTY

Hey, it's the brains.

GEORGE

Even if you're smart . . .

ALEX

Little technical screw-up tonight, Dennis?
(DENNIS *exits*)

GEORGE

You think it's all together,
And something falls apart . . .

170

(Music continues under)

BETTY

I love the new machine, George.

GEORGE

Thanks. That means a lot to me.

ALEX

We saw you talking to Redmond from Texas.

GEORGE

Yeah.

BETTY

Did you get one of the commissions?

GEORGE

We talked about it. You guys?

ALEX

Her. My stuff is a little too inaccessible.

GEORGE

I love your work, Alex. I'll put in a good word for you.

ALEX
(Defensive)

He knows my work!

GEORGE
(Uncomfortable)

It's all politics, Alex. Maybe if you just lightened up once in a while.

BETTY

(*Mollifying*)

Texas would be fun!

(GEORGE *beckons and a fourth cut-out slides in and heads toward* BETTY *and* ALEX)

GEORGE

(*Front*)

Art isn't easy.

(*Gesturing towards* ALEX)

Overnight you're a trend

You're the right combination —

(*Behind him, cut-out #1 begins sinking slowly into the floor*)

Then the trend's at an end,

You're suddenly last year's sensation . . .

(*Notices the cut-out, goes to raise it during the following*)

So you should support the competition,

Try to set aside your own ambition,

Even while you jockey for position —

(*Cut-out #4 has slid in too far, and* BETTY *and* ALEX *have turned away;* GEORGE, *unflustered, spins it back around towards* BETTY *and* ALEX, *who resume talking to it*)

If you feel a sense of coalition,

Then you never really stand alone.

If you want your work to reach fruition,

What you need's a link with your tradition,

And of course a prominent commission,

(*Cut-out #1 starts to sink again;* GEORGE *hastens to fix it*)

Plus a little formal recognition,
So that you can go on exhibit —
            (*Getting flustered*)
So that your work can go on exhibition —
    (*Loud promenade, very brief, during which cut-out #1
    starts to go again, but stops just as* GEORGE *reaches
    it. As* HE *does so,* BLAIR DANIELS, *an art critic, comes
    up to him. Chords under*)

BLAIR

There's the man of the hour.

GEORGE

Blair. Hello. I just read your piece on Neo-Expressionism —

BLAIR

Just what the world needs — another piece on Neo-Expressionism.

GEORGE

Well, I enjoyed it.
            (*Chords continue under, irregularly*)

BLAIR

Good for you! Now, I had no idea you might be related to nine-
teenth-century France.

GEORGE

It's a cloudy ancestral line at best.

BLAIR

I'm dying to meet your grandmother. It was fun seeing the two
of you onstage with your invention. It added a certain humanity
to the proceedings.

173

GEORGE

Humanity?

BLAIR

George. Chromolume Number Seven?

GEORGE

Be nice, George . . .
 (*Gestures for a cut-out; it doesn't rise*)

BLAIR

I was hoping it would be a series of three — four at the most.

GEORGE

You have to pay a price, George . . .
 (*Gestures again; nothing*)

BLAIR

We have been there before, you know.

GEORGE

You never suffer from a shortage of opinions, do you, Blair?

BLAIR

You never minded my opinions when they were in your favor!

BLAIR	GEORGE
I have touted your work from	They like to give
the beginning, you know	Advice, George —
that. You were really on	(*Gestures offstage; nothing*)
to something with these	Don't think about it
light machines — once.	Twice, George . . .
Now they're just becoming	(*Gestures again; nothing*)

174

more and more about less
and less.

GEORGE

I disagree.

> (*Music.* BLAIR *turns briefly away from him, rummaging through her purse for a cigarette.* GEORGE *takes advantage of this to rush offstage and bring on cutout #5, which* HE *sets up in front of her during the following*)

BLAIR

Don't get me wrong. You're a talented guy. If you weren't, I wouldn't waste our time with my opinions. I think you are capable of far more. Not that you couldn't succeed by doing Chromolume after Chromolume — but there are new discoveries to be made, George.

> (SHE *holds up her cigarette and waits for a light from the cut-out*)

GEORGE

Be new, George.
They tell you till they're blue, George:
You're new or else you're through, George,
And even if it's true, George —
You do what you can do . . .
> (*Wandering among cut-outs, checking them*)
Bit by bit,
Putting it together.
Piece by piece,
Working out the vision night and day.
All it takes is time and perseverance,
With a little luck along the way,

175

Putting in a personal appearance,
Gathering supporters and adherents . . .
(Music stops. BLAIR, *getting impatient for her light, leaves the cut-out to join another group.* GEORGE *notices. Beat)*

HARRIET
(To BILLY)
. . . But he combines all these different trends . . .
(Beat. The cut-out with HARRIET *and* BILLY *falters)*

GEORGE
(Moving to it smoothly as music resumes)
Mapping out the right configuration,
(Adjusting it)
Starting with a suitable foundation . . .

BETTY
. . . He's an original . . .

ALEX
. . . Was . . .
(During the following, all the cut-outs falter sporadically, causing GEORGE *to move more and more rapidly among them)*

GEORGE
Lining up a prominent commission —
And an exhibition in addition —
Here a little dab of politician —
There a little touch of publication —
Till you have a balanced composition —

Everything depends on preparation —
Even if you do have the suspicion
That it's taking all your concentration —

(*Simultaneously, with* GEORGE)

BETTY

I like those images.

ALEX

Some.

BETTY

They're just his personal response.

ALEX

To what?

BETTY

The painting!

ALEX

Bullshit. Anyway, the painting's overrated . . .

BETTY

Overrated? It's a masterpiece!

ALEX

A masterpiece? Historically important maybe —

BETTY

Oh, now you're judging Seurat, are you?

177

ALEX

All it is is pleasant, just like George's work.

BETTY

It's just your jealousy of George's work.

ALEX

No nuance, no resonance, no relevance —

BETTY

There's nuance and there's resonance, there's relevance —

ALEX

There's not much point in arguing.
Besides, it's all promotion, but then —

BETTY

There's not much point in arguing.
You say it's all promotion, but then —

GREENBERG

It's only new, though, for now
And yesterday's forgotten.
Today it's all a matter of promotion,
But then —

REDMOND

Nouveau.
And yesterday's forgotten
And you can't tell good from rotten
And today it's all a matter of promotion,
But then —

178

HARRIET

You can't divide art today.
Go with it!
What will they think of next?

BILLY

I'm not surprised.
What will they think of next?

OTHERS

Most art today
Is a matter of promotion, but then —

GEORGE	ALL
The art of making art	
Is putting it together —	That is the state of the art
Bit by bit —	
Link by link —	
Drink by drink —	
Mink by mink —	And art isn't easy.
And that	
Is the state	
Of the	

ALL

Art!

(GEORGE *frames the successfully completed picture with
his hands, as at the end of Act I. As soon as* HE *exits,
however, the cut-outs collapse and disappear.* MARIE
and ELAINE *are over at the painting;* THEY *are joined
by* HARRIET *and* BILLY)

179

GREENBERG
Ladies and gentlemen, dinner is served.
(*Most of the party exits*)

HARRIET
(*To* MARIE)
Excuse me, could you please tell me: what is that square form up there?

BLAIR
(*Who has been standing nearby*)
That is a baby carriage.

MARIE
Who told you that?!

BLAIR
I'm sorry to butt in. I'm Blair Daniels and I've been waiting for the opportunity to tell you how much I enjoyed seeing you on stage.

MARIE
Why, thank you. But, my dear, that is not a baby carriage. That is Louis' waffle stove.

BLAIR
Waffle stove? I've read all there is to read about this work, and there's never been any mention of a waffle stove!

MARIE
(*Indicating red book*)
I have a book, too. My mother's. It is a family legacy, as is this painting. And my mother often spoke of Louis' waffle stove!

180

BLAIR

Louis. Yes, you mentioned him in your presentation.
(GEORGE *re-enters; stays off to one side*)

MARIE

Family. You know, it is all you really have.

BILLY

You said that before.

MARIE

I say it often.

HARRIET

Excuse us.
(HARRIET *and* BILLY *exit*)

MARIE

You know, Miss Daniels, there are only two worthwhile things to leave behind when you depart this world: children and art. Isn't that correct?

BLAIR

I never quite thought of it that way.
(ELAINE *joins them*)

MARIE

Do you know Elaine?

BLAIR

No. I don't believe we've met. Blair Daniels.

ELAINE

I've heard a lot about you.

181

BLAIR

Oh, yes.

MARIE

Elaine and George were married once. I was so excited. I thought *they* might have a child. George and I are the only ones left, I'm afraid.

(*Whispers*)

I want George to have a child — continue the line. You can understand that, can't you, Elaine?

ELAINE

Of course.

MARIE

Are you married, Miss Daniels?

BLAIR

Awfully nice to have met you.

(SHE *shakes* MARIE's *hand and exits*)

MARIE

Elaine, fix my chair so I can see Mama.

(SHE *does*. ELAINE *crosses to* GEORGE)

ELAINE

George. I think Marie is a little too tired for the party. She seems to be slipping a bit.

GEORGE

I better take her back to the hotel.

ELAINE

I'll take her back. You stay.

182

GEORGE

Nah, it's a perfect excuse for me to leave early.

ELAINE

George. Don't be silly! You're the toast of the party. You should feel wonderful.

GEORGE
(*Edgy*)

Well, I don't feel wonderful.

ELAINE

Poor George. Well . . . tonight was a wonderful experience for Marie. I don't remember seeing her so happy. It was very good of you to include her.

GEORGE

She is something, isn't she?

ELAINE

Yes, she is . . .
> (ELAINE *begins to leave*; GEORGE *stops her*; THEY *embrace. Then* SHE *exits. The preceding has been underscored with the chords from Act I.* MARIE *has been staring up at the painting*)

MARIE
(*Sings*)

You would have liked him,
Mama, you would.
Mama, he makes things —
Mama, they're good.
Just as you said from the start:
Children and art . . .

183

(Starts nodding off)

Children and art . . .

He should be happy —
Mama, he's blue.
What do I do?

You should have seen it,
It was a sight!
Mama, I mean it —
All color and light — !
I don't understand what it was,
But, Mama, the things that he does —
They twinkle and shimmer and buzz —
You would have liked them . . .
It . . .
Him . . .

(Music continues)

Henry . . . Henry? . . . Henry . . .

GEORGE

(Coming over)

It's George, Grandmother.

MARIE

Of course it is. I thought you were your father for a moment.
(Indicating painting)
Did I tell you who that was?

GEORGE

Of course. That is your mother.

MARIE

That is correct.

184

(Sings)
Isn't she beautiful?
There she is —
　　　　(Pointing to different figures)
There she is, there she is, there she is —
Mama is everywhere,
He must have loved her so much . . .

　　　　　　GEORGE
Is she really in all those places, Marie?

　　　　　　MARIE
This is our family —
This is the lot.
After I go, this is
All that you've got, honey —

　　　　　　GEORGE
Now, let's not have this discussion —

　　　　　　MARIE
Wasn't she beautiful, though?

You would have liked her.
Mama did things
No one had done.

Mama was funny,
Mama was fun,
Mama spent money
When she had none.
Mama said, "Honey,
Mustn't be blue.
It's not so much do what you like

185

As it is that you like what you do."
Mama said, "Darling,
Don't make such a drama.
A little less thinking,
A little more feeling—"

GEORGE

Please don't start—

MARIE

I'm just quoting Mama . . .
            (*Interrupting, indicates* LOUISE)
The child is so sweet . . .
            (*Indicates the* CELESTES *at center*)
And the girls are so rapturous . . .
Isn't it lovely how artists can capture us?

GEORGE

Yes, it is, Marie.

MARIE

You would have liked her—
Honey, I'm wrong,
You would have loved her.

Mama enjoyed things.
Mama was smart.
See how she shimmers—
I mean from the heart.
            (ELAINE *enters and stands off to the side*)
I know, honey, you don't agree,
                    (*Indicates painting*)

186

But this is our family tree.
Just wait till we're there, and you'll see —
Listen to me . . .
>   (*Drifting off*)
Mama was smart . . .
Listen to Mama . . .
Children and art . . .
Children and art . . .
>   (*She falls asleep and* ELAINE *crosses to her and wheels her off. As* THEY *go:*)
Goodbye, Mama.
>   (GEORGE *looks at the painting for a moment*)

GEORGE
Connect, George. Connect . . .
>   (GEORGE *exits; the painting flies out*)

(*The island is once again revealed, though barely recognizable as the trees have been replaced by high-rise buildings. The only tree still visible is the one in front of which the* OLD LADY *and* NURSE *sat.* DENNIS *kneels, studying his blueprints.* GEORGE *enters, camera in hand*)

GEORGE
Are you certain this is the best place for the Chromolume?

DENNIS
George, this is the largest clearing on La Grande Jatte.

GEORGE
Where's the still?

187

DENNIS

It has been built and should arrive tomorrow morning a few hours before the Chromolume. I wanted it here today, but they don't make deliveries on Sunday.

GEORGE

And fresh water for the cooling system?

DENNIS

We can draw it from the Seine. As for the electricity —

GEORGE

Did you see this tree?

DENNIS

No.

GEORGE

It could be the one in the painting.

DENNIS

Yes. It could.
(GEORGE *hands* DENNIS *the camera and goes to the tree.* DENNIS *takes a picture of him in front of it*)

GEORGE

At least something is recognizable . . . Now, about the electricity?

DENNIS

The wind generator's over there.

GEORGE

You have been efficient, as always.

DENNIS

Thank you.

GEORGE

I will miss working with you, Dennis.

DENNIS

Well, I can recommend some very capable people to help you with the Texas commission.

GEORGE

I turned it down.

DENNIS

What?

GEORGE

Dennis, why are you quitting?

DENNIS

I told you, I want —

GEORGE

I know what you told me! Why are you really leaving?

DENNIS

George. I love the Chromolumes. But I've helped you build the last five, and now I want to do something different.

GEORGE

I wish you had told me that in the first place.

DENNIS

I'm sorry.

GEORGE

Why do you think I turned down the commission? I don't want to do the same thing over and over again either.

DENNIS

There are other things you could do.

GEORGE

I know that. I just want to do something I care about.
(*Beat.* GEORGE *puts camera in pocket and pulls out* DOT*'s red book*)

DENNIS

I see you brought the red book.

GEORGE

Since Marie has died, I thought I would at least bring something of hers along.

DENNIS

Marie really wanted to make this trip.

GEORGE

I know.

DENNIS

I hope you don't mind, but I took a look at the book. It's very interesting.

GEORGE

It's just a grammar book, Dennis.

DENNIS
(*Imploring*)

Not that part. The notes in the back.

(GEORGE *leafs through it to the back*)
Well, we just have to wait for it to get dark. I'm not certain about the ambient light.

GEORGE
You go, Dennis. I'd like to be alone actually.

DENNIS

Are you sure?

GEORGE
Yeah. I'll see you back at the hotel.
(HE *sits on the ground*)

DENNIS
(*Begins to exit*)
George. I look forward to seeing what you come up with next.

GEORGE
(*Smiling*)
You're not the only one, Dennis.
(DENNIS *exits. Music.* GEORGE *sings, leafing through the book, reading*)
"Charles has a book . . ."
(*Turns a page*)
"Charles shows them his crayons . . ."
(*Turns back a few pages*)
"Marie has the ball of Charles . . ."
(*Turns the book to read writing in the margin*)
"Good for Marie . . ."
(*Smiles at the coincidence of the name, turns a page*)
"Charles misses his ball . . ."
(*Looks up*)
George misses Marie . . .

191

George misses a lot . . .
George is alone.

George looks around.
He sees the park.
It is depressing.
George looks ahead.
George sees the dark.
George is afraid.
Where are the people
Out strolling on Sunday?

George looks within:
George is adrift.
George goes by guessing.
George looks behind:
He had a gift.
When did it fade?
You wanted people out
Strolling on Sunday —
Sorry, Marie. . . .
        (*Looks again at the name in the book*)
See George remember how George used to be,
Stretching his vision in every direction.
See George attempting to see a connection
When all he can see
Is maybe a tree —
                (*Humorously*)
The family tree —
Sorry, Marie . . .

George is afraid.
George sees the park.

192

George sees it dying.
George too may fade,
Leaving no mark,
Just passing through.
Just like the people
Out strolling on Sunday . . .

George looks around.
George is alone.
No use denying
George is aground.
George has outgrown
What he can do.
George would have liked to see
People out strolling on Sunday . . .
> (DOT *appears.* GEORGE *looks up and discovers* HER. HE
> *stands*)

DOT

I almost did not recognize you without your beard. You have
my book.

GEORGE

Your book?

DOT

Yes.

GEORGE

It is a little difficult to understand.

DOT

Well, I was teaching myself. My writing got much better. I
worked very hard. I made certain that Marie learned right away.

193

GEORGE
(*Looks at the book*)

Marie . . .

DOT

It is good to see you. Not that I ever forgot you, George. You gave me so much.

GEORGE

What did I give you?

DOT

Oh, many things. You taught me about concentration. At first I thought that meant just being still, but I was to understand it meant much more. You meant to tell me to be where I was — not some place in the past or future. I worried too much about tomorrow. I thought the world could be perfect. I was wrong.

GEORGE

What else?

DOT

Oh, enough about me. What about you? Are you working on something new?

GEORGE

No. I am not working on anything new.
(*Music begins*)

DOT

That is not like you, George.

GEORGE
(*Sings*)
I've nothing to say.

DOT
You have many things . . .

GEORGE
Well, nothing that's not been said.

DOT
(*Sings*)
Said by you, though, George . . .

GEORGE
I do not know where to go.

DOT
And nor did I.

GEORGE
I want to make things that count,
Things that will be new . . .

DOT
I did what I had to do:

GEORGE
What am I to do?

DOT
Move on.
Stop worrying where you're going —

Move on.
If you can know where you're going,
You've gone.
Just keep moving on.

I chose, and my world was shaken —
So what?
The choice may have been mistaken,
The choosing was not.
You have to move on.

Look at what you want,
Not at where you are,
Not at what you'll be.
Look at all the things you've done for me:

Opened up my eyes,
Taught me how to see,
Notice every tree —

GEORGE

. . . Notice every tree . . .

DOT

Understand the light —

GEORGE

. . . Understand the light. . .

DOT

Concentrate on now —

196

I want to move on.
I want to explore the light.
I want to know how to get through,
Through to something new,
Something of my own —

GEORGE *and* DOT

Move on.
Move on.

DOT

Stop worrying if your vision
Is new.
Let others make that decision —
They usually do.
You keep moving on.

(*Simultaneously*)

DOT	GEORGE
Look at what you've done,	(*Looking around*)
	. . . Something in the light,
Then at what you want,	Something in the sky,
Not at where you are,	In the grass,
What you'll be.	Up behind the trees . . .
Look at all the things	
You gave to me.	Things I hadn't looked at
Let me give to you	Till now:
Something in return.	Flower on your hat.
I would be so pleased . . .	And your smile.

GEORGE

And the color of your hair.
And the way you catch the light.

197

And the care.
And the feeling.
And the life
Moving on.

We've always belonged
Together!

We will always belong
Together!

Just keep moving on.

Anything you do,
Let it come from you.
Then it will be new.
Give us more to see . . .

You never cared what anyone thought. That upset me at the
time because I wanted you to care what *I* thought.

I'm sure that I did.

I am sure that you did, too.

Dot.

(HE *takes book to* DOT)

Why did you write these words?

DOT

They are your words, George. The ones you muttered so often when you worked.

GEORGE
(Reads slowly)

"Order."

(Chord. OLD LADY enters)

OLD LADY

George. Is that you?
 (GEORGE turns to her. HE looks back to DOT, who smiles,
 then back to the OLD LADY)

GEORGE

Yes.

OLD LADY

Tell me! Is this place as you expected it?

GEORGE

What?

OLD LADY

The park, of course.

GEORGE

Somewhat.

OLD LADY

Go on.

199

GEORGE

Well, the greens are a little darker. The sky a little greyer. Mud tones in the water.

OLD LADY
(*Disappointed*)

Well, yes, I suppose —

GEORGE

But the air is rich and full of light.

OLD LADY

Good.
(*Chord. As the* OLD LADY *leaves,* GEORGE *reads the next word:*)

GEORGE

"Design."
(*Music begins: "Sunday." The downstage right building begins to rise. The* CELESTES *appear and begin to cross the stage*)
"Tension."
(*Two buildings rise stage right and left. More* CHARACTERS *from the painting appear and begin to promenade*)
"Composition."
(*Building rises*)
"Balance."
(*Buildings rise. The stage is filled by the* CHARACTERS *from the painting*)
"Light."
(*The large building in the back rises*)
Dot. I cannot read this word.

"Harmony."

ALL (*Sing*)	GEORGE (*Reading again, struggling with the words*)

Sunday,
By the blue
Purple yellow red water
On the green
Purple yellow red grass,
As we pass
Through arrangements of
           shadows
Towards the verticals of trees
Forever
   (ALL *bow to* GEORGE)
By the blue
Purple yellow red water
On the green
Orange violet mass
Of the grass
	"So much love in his words
	. . . forever with his colors
	. . . how George looks . . .
	he can look forever . . . what
	does he see? . . . his eyes so
	dark and shiny . . . so careful
	. . . so exact. . . ."
	(DOT *takes* GEORGE *by the arm
	and turns him to the group*)

DOT

  In our perfect park,

GEORGE

  Made of flecks of light
  And dark,

ALL
(*Except* GEORGE *and* DOT)

And parasols . . .
People strolling through the trees

Of a small suburban park
On an island in the river
On an ordinary Sunday . . .

(*The* COMPANY *has settled in the areas that* THEY *occupy in the painting*)

Sunday

(ALL *begin to leave very slowly, except* DOT, *who remains downstage with* GEORGE)

Sunday . . .

(DOT *leaves* GEORGE, *crossing upstage into the park;* SHE *turns toward* GEORGE. *The white canvas drop descends*)

GEORGE
(*Reading from the book*)
"White. A blank page or canvas. His favorite. So many possibilities . . ."

(HE *looks up and sees* DOT *disappearing behind the white canvas. Lights fade to black*)

The following, delivered by the first-act George, was cut in previews.

GEORGE
*(Enters downstage and stands on the apron in front
of the tableau)*

A fascination with light. The bedroom where I slept as a child — it had a window. At night, the reflection of the light — that is, the light outside the window — created a shadow-show on my wall. So it was, lying in my bed, looking at the wall, I was able to make out shapes of night activity from the street. These images were not rich in detail, so my mind's eye filled in the shapes to bring them to life. Straying from the point. The point? Light and sleep. I didn't sleep. Well, of course I slept, but always when there was a choice, when I might fight the urge, I would lie awake, eyes fixed on the wall, sometimes until the bright sunlight of the morning washed the image away.

Off and running. Off and running. First into the morning light. Last on the gas-lit streets. Energy that had no time for sleep. A mission to see, to record impressions. Seeing . . . recording . . . seeing the record, then feeling the experience. Connect the dots, George.

Slowing to a screeching halt — in one week. Fighting to wake up. "Wake up, Georgie." I can still feel her cool hand on my warm cheek. Could darkness be an inviting place? Could sleep surpass off and running? No. Lying still, I can see the boys swimming in the Seine. I can see them all, on a sunny Sunday in the park.

(HE *exits*)